RIGGING

Enrico Sala

W·W·NORTON & COMPANY
New York   London

ISBN 0-393-03324-4

W. W. Norton & Company, Inc., 500 Fifth Avenue, New York, NY 10110
W. W. Norton & Company, Ltd., 37 Great Russell Street, London WC1B 3NU

Printed and bound by South China Ptg Co., Hong Kong

1 2 3 4 5 6 7 8 9 0

CONTENTS

CONTENTS

INTRODUCTION

I first made Enrico's acquaintance over the telephone. He wanted to go around the world on the *B&B Italia* and asked me to put in a good word for him. He did not know that I was in the same position! I told him that the boat was at Lavagna, at the Sangermani yard, and that in my opinion the best move would be to go there in person. At the end of the following week we met at the yard – and Enrico remained on board *B&B* from that moment until the end of the trip.

Neither of us had had a great deal of experience, although we both had sailed a bit: Enrico on a cruising yacht to the Caribbean and I in the usual regattas (the ones which in those days we organised ourselves) and in a Cape-to-Rio, with the subsequent return voyage to Italy. Enrico was no professional racing sailor and, for that matter, neither was I. All we wanted to do was to sail, be at sea, go around the world, live under sail.

Enrico immediately proved to be exceptionally nimble-fingered and quick on the uptake; he managed to do everything well (even jobs he had never done before) and, what was more, he got better every time he did it. He used his head and was never in a hurry to finish a job, but was determined that the work should be done exactly as he envisaged it.

This first round-the-world trip was a very important experience for us. We were a homogeneous group, without any 'stars', and our skipper, Corrado de Majo, had complete confidence in us and interfered as little as possible. As planned, I disembarked at Rio while Enrico remained on board until the boat reached England and also (if I remember rightly) returned with her to Italy.

We have run into each other frequently since then over the past ten years. Not that we have done everything together: far from it, but many things we have. We have even met by chance in places where we had arrived independently, each on his own mission, and at once got together and hatched out some combined project. Afterwards we went our separate ways again, certain nonetheless that our paths would inevitably cross once more.

So it was that Enrico arrived in England shortly before my first trimaran, *Blueamnesya*, was launched and gave me a hand in getting her to the Sound of Rhum. Another time, we ran into each other unexpectedly in Miami, Enrico on *Kialoa* and I on another trimaran, *Rusty Pelican*, which we took to Venice together to compete in the 500 × 2. Our last sailing adventure together was on *Star Point*, a trimaran built entirely by ourselves.

Generally it is the publisher who asks someone to write the introduction to a book; but in this case it was I who suggested it. The proofs, when I read them, brought back ten years of sailing and sea and, in a flash of courage (and with a certain lack of modesty), I found myself saying 'I'll write the introduction myself'.

Each chapter of this book brings to mind episodes from real life. There is not one piece of advice given which does not come from direct experience. The recommendations may appear just too simple at first sight, but in fact this is far from the case. Behind them are months of sailing, of work in yards and sail lofts and, of course, of repairs carried out and tested while at sea. They are invaluable hints which will save much time, energy and money both in the preparation of the craft before launching and afterwards in sailing her.

I recognise in these pages the meticulousness of Enrico, his unfailing attention to detail, his dislike of unnecessary frills. I am sure that this will be an extremely useful book for all those who, in one way or another, love sailing – from the ordinary weekend sailor, to the charterer, to the out-and-out racing enthusiast. I can recommend it highly as a competent book written by an experienced sailor who really knows what he is talking about.

PAOLO MARTINONI

1. THE DECK

The deck of your boat, whether plastic or luxurious teak, should always be kept in good order, both for practical and for aesthetic reasons. Like the fair sex, no self-respecting yacht likes to appear in public dishevelled and tousled; it is up to you to see that she does not cut a poor figure among her companions at the quayside.

The deck should be washed down after every cruise with plenty of fresh water to remove all traces of salt spray. A more thorough maintenance programme should be carried out twice a year, at the end and at the beginning of the sailing season; the more care you take when laying up your boat, the fewer will be the problems when you start sailing again.

PLASTIC DECKS

There are various types of plastic deck. Some boats have moulded decks, with suitable patterns impressed on the moulds so that the surface of catwalks and work-areas is rough and will not be slippery when wet. These decks only need periodic scrubbing down with a large brush and well-diluted detergent, plus a little Jif and a hard sponge at those points where dirt has caked. Jif is also excellent for cleaning fenders, but it must be used lightly on bright metal surfaces since it is mildly abrasive.

Other plastic boats, however, which are not mass-produced, have decks that are produced by a different technique, necessitating the application of non-slip deck paint. This type of paint usually consists of a normal polyurethane varnish mixed with a special powder that, when the varnish has dried, gives the deck a surface with the character of sandpaper. If you cannot obtain the special powder, you can use fine well-dried sand equally well or, indeed, any other similar substance which you think suitable as roughening agent. Once I even used sugar with, I may say, quite satisfactory results.

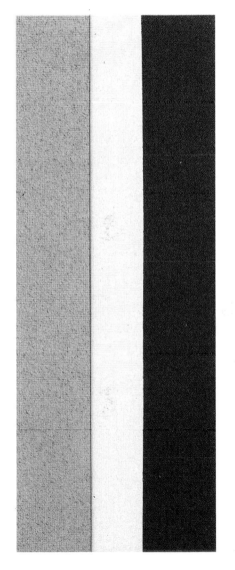

Different types of non-slip surface. The material shown above is sufficiently soft and not too heavy, compared with the classic Treadmaster (*on opposite page*) which is extremely effective but somewhat heavy and has a surface which is very rough on the clothes and bare skin of the crew. Both types are applied with special bonding agents and are used in particular on steel and light-alloy boats. Whenever possible, it is best to use non-slip deck paints which are not only lighter, but cheap and easy to apply.

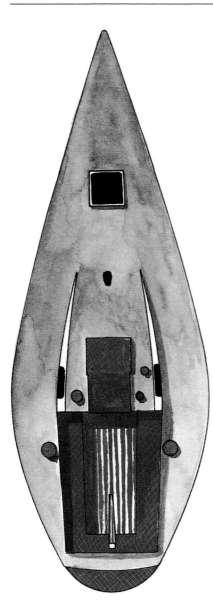

Any glossy areas of the deck which have become slightly matt can be restored by applying a liquid abrasive with a swab of cotton wool, followed by rubbing with polish.

WOODEN DECKS

The procedure becomes more complex if your boat has a teak deck. Teak has exceptional qualities but, contrary to wide-spread belief, it also requires maintenance and up-keep if it is not to acquire a drab grey colour which makes the boat look old and shabby. If the deck is of fairly recent construction, it can be given a 'beauty treatment' using an American product called Teak Brite. The treatment consists of three separate stages: cleaning, brightening of the planking, varnishing with a petroleum-based sealing varnish. The materials to be used at each stage are supplied by the manufacturer together with instructions for their application. The entire treatment requires from three to five hours' work, preferably choosing a clear sunny day, and should be repeated at the beginning of each sailing season – or at least every two years.

If the teak planking is old and weathered or has deep ruts, the deck will have to be rubbed down with a portable orbital sander, using a fine (100–150 grade) abrasive. Be careful, though, not to go too deep: the teak has to last for many years to come! To finish the treatment, apply a couple of coats of Teak Brite sealing varnish; these will protect the deck from normal wear and tear and enable it to keep its attractive pale colour.

Decks so treated should be washed down frequently (without using hard brushes or detergents), particularly after each cruise, to remove all traces of salt spray.

Deckhouses, washboards, coamings and other deck structures protected with yacht varnish should be inspected every year. If they are in good condition, one coat of yacht varnish will be enough after rubbing down the surface lightly with very fine (220–280 grade) sandpaper. If, on the other hand, the varnish has been neglected and is clearly defective with bad cracks and blisters, it may have to be removed entirely. This is done with a paint-remover and a scraper (or a small piece of glass with a straight edge, to be used, with due care, until it is blunted). After stripping down to the bare wood, apply a well-thinned (50 per cent)

A teak deck in perfect condition. *Left*: a piece of glass with padded grip for preparing surface for varnishing. The old varnish should be removed completely with a scraper (sharpened periodically with a file) and with the help of paint-remover. If a scraper is not available, a piece of glass with a straight edge will do equally well. The paint-remover should be used with caution. *On opposite page*: radar-reflecting paint. This system can be used on boats which have painted decks and has proved to be very effective. The selected paint is mixed with a special compound containing very fine aluminium dust. When the paint is dry, the entire deck acts as a radar-reflector.

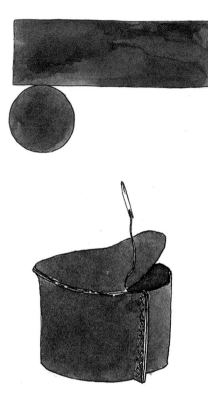

first coat of yacht varnish to prime the wood and then continue with six to ten coats, rubbing down the surface lightly between one coat and the next.

LEAKS

A leaking deck is an irritating defect which can ruin a holiday or take all the pleasure out of a sailing weekend. The first thing to do is to trace the leak to its source, removing if necessary the cabin interior panelling so as to have direct access to the underside of the deck planking. Some through-bolt securing a stanchion, a rail, a pulpit or (more rarely) a winch is generally to blame and the leak can be stopped by removing the bolt, clearing the hole and refitting the bolt well-smeared with a suitable type of sealing compound, eg Sikaflex, red-lead putty or, if you cannot find anything better, normal transparent marine varnish. Remember, however, that the most effective sealing compounds for through-bolts are those which never harden completely.

If the trouble is a skylight or hatch which is not entirely watertight, check the hinges and rubber seal and replace these if necessary.

Compass cover. The damping liquid in the compass consists of a mixture of alcohol, glycerine and distilled water which, after prolonged exposure to the sun, tends to become cloudy, making it difficult to read the card. This can be avoided by protecting the compass with a hood made of medium heavy canvas, tailored and sewn by hand (or by machine) on the inside, using a sailmaker's needle and thread. The pattern is shown at the top.

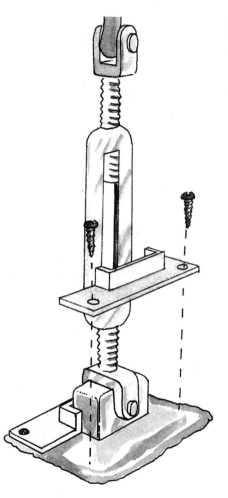

Cover plate for chain plate. It is essential that the cover plate fits closely around the chain plate and that the sealing compound is applied liberally to all contact surfaces.

Other measures are required instead if the leak is around the chain plates. In this case, a special small steel plate must be obtained which surrounds the fastenings and is then fixed to the deck with wood screws; installation is completed with the usual sealing compound. These special plates can be found at most yacht chandlers (the American firm Schaefer, for example, produces a whole range of different models and sizes) or you can have them made to measure by any machine-shop that handles stainless steel components. Obviously, you will have to undo the standing rigging in order to install the plates; however, if you undo one shroud (or stay) at a time, there will be no danger to the mast and you will also have the chance to carry out that oft-considered re-tensioning operation (see Chapter 3).

PULPIT AND LIFELINES

Pulpits and lifelines should be inspected at frequent intervals, since they are both equally essential for safety on deck. The pulpit (and pushpit) should be anchored firmly to the deck and should be strong enough to bear the weight of a person without bending or swaying. Openings must be closed with bars or ropes when at sea. It is also advisable to wind non-slip tape around any sections of the pulpit or pushpit where you put your feet either when entering or leaving the boat, or when struggling with the spinnaker boom.

Lifelines must be kept sufficiently taut. At the forward end they should be connected to the eye of the pulpit in the least cumbersome possible manner, since on broad reaches the genoa tends to rub against that particular point. As a rule, the lifelines are tightened aft by means of the small turnbuckles with which they are secured to the pushpit. If the turnbuckle is fully tightened and the line is still slack, there is a simple

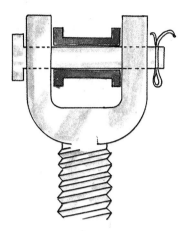

Above: Teflon insulator bush for lifelines. To eliminate the 'Faraday Cage' effect, a bush can be inserted that interrupts the electrical circuit between lifeline and pulpit.
Below: lanyard for tightening lifelines in place of turnbuckle. Use a stout 4–6 mm line; the number of loops depends on the size of the wire.

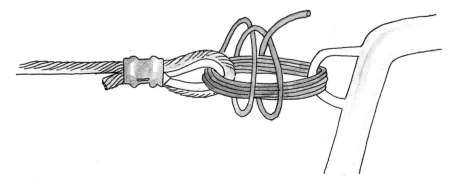

remedy: remove the fitting and splice or Talurit an eye around a thimble, in the end of the wire. Lash this to the pulpit eye by passing a lanyard through both of them ten times or more, draw the lashing tight and make fast with half hitches. This solution is easy, economical, safe and not least important non-conductive. It should, in fact, not be forgotten that the continuous all-steel system formed by pulpits and guardrails can act as a kind of 'Faraday Cage' around the boat, interfering with radio communications and, in particu-

lar, with radio direction finders.

The bow section of the guardrail can be fitted with lacing that prevents the foresails falling overboard when lowered. When small children are on board it is advisable to fit fine-mesh netting all around the gunwale.

Pulpits, stanchions, winches and any other stainless steel deck fittings can be cleaned and polished with excellent results using either Wenol or a very fine grinding paste.

Many people who pride themselves on being 'old seadogs' con-

sider deck cleaning and maintenance as being activities reserved for 'armchair sailors'. Nothing could be further from the truth! Quite apart from the obvious satisfaction of having your boat always in perfect trim, cleaning and maintaining give you an opportunity for periodically checking many critical points in the mast and deck fittings and for discovering potential trouble spots that would escape notice during a more cursory examination.

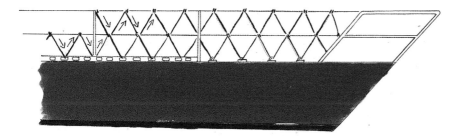

Lifeline lacing. Hitch a 4–5 mm line to the upper line at the point where stay meets stanchion. Complete upper portion first, lashing line with a clove hitch each time it meets the upper and middle stays; for lower portion, thread line alternately through the holes in the toerail and over the hitch on the middle stay. In this way, the lower portion can be removed easily when necessary for working on deck.

Leather protective covers

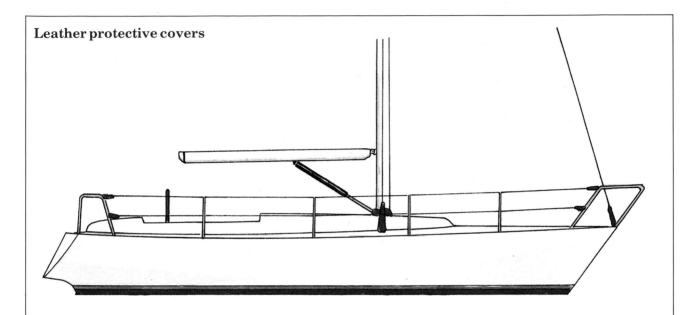

Leather sheathing serves the purpose of protecting specific parts of the running rigging which are more exposed to wear and tear (sails, sheets, halyards, lifts etc); they also greatly improve the look of the boat. With a flexible tape measure, measure the exact overall dimensions of the item to be covered. Transfer the measurements and draw the outline of the item on the back of the leather with a biro and with the help of a set square; allow a margin of 0.5 in (1 cm) all round which is folded back and glued with a Bostik type of adhesive. Punch a series of evenly spaced holes on both sides of the sheath with a hole-puncher, taking care that holes on opposite sides are perfectly aligned. Wrap the cover around the item and sew the edges together, using two sailmaker's needles (size 17) and waxed twine. The stitches are made by passing each needle in turn from the inside to the outside and crossing over between each set of holes. Use calf hide for the sheathing.

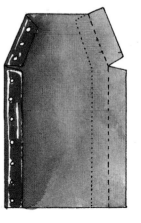

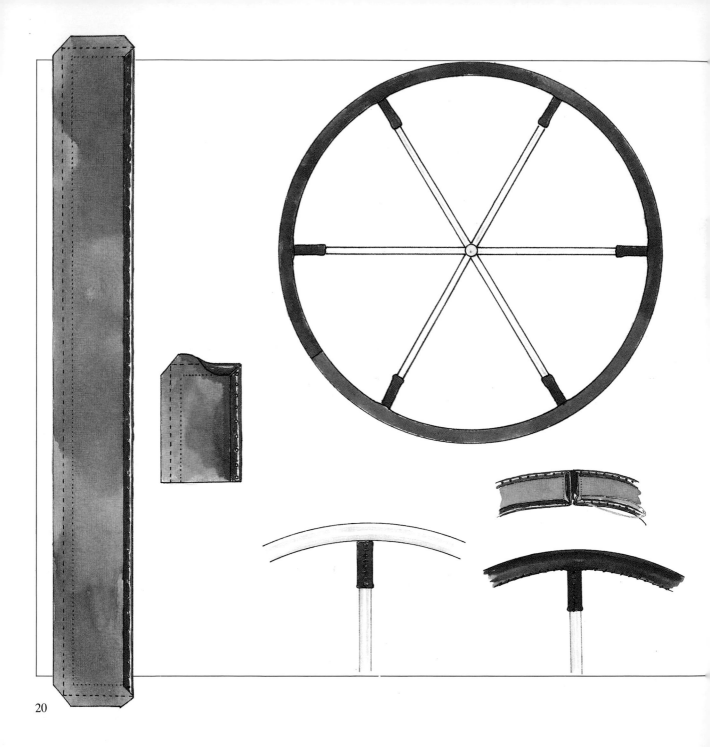

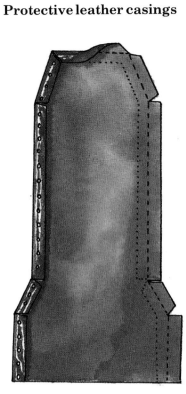

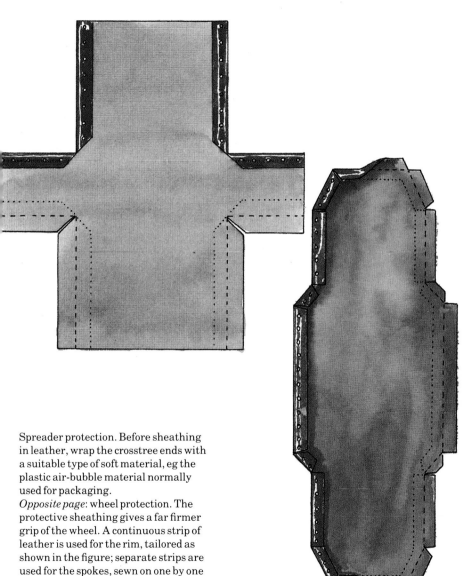

Spreader protection. Before sheathing in leather, wrap the crosstree ends with a suitable type of soft material, eg the plastic air-bubble material normally used for packaging.

Opposite page: wheel protection. The protective sheathing gives a far firmer grip of the wheel. A continuous strip of leather is used for the rim, tailored as shown in the figure; separate strips are used for the spokes, sewn on one by one

before sheathing the rim. All strips are sewn with usual cross-stitch technique using, in the case of the rim, continuous lengths of thread between each pair of spokes. All parts to be sheathed must first be wrapped with double-sided adhesive tape, which serves to anchor the leather to the underlying surface and to off-set the tendency of leather to stretch and slacken when wet.

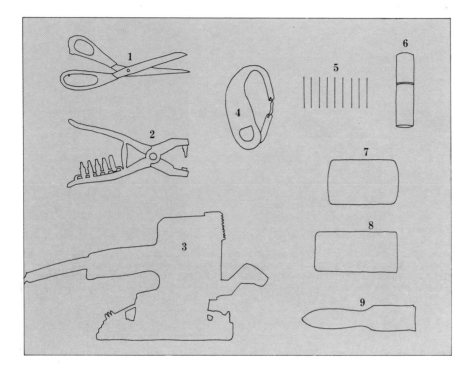

1. The most suitable on the market are made by Wilkinson. **2.** Choose a rugged heavy-duty model with a set of interchangeable hollow punches (wheel models are not recommended). **3.** There are several makes on the market; choose the model that best meets your requirements for size and output power. **4.** Check that the palm is not too soft and that it fits comfortably onto your hand; if necessary, the width can be adjusted by inserting a length of string. **5/6.** It is very difficult to keep needles on board free of rust. Commonly used preventive measures are grease (vaseline-type), coffee beans, talcum powder, etc. What is essential is a good airtight container (most effective are plastic medicine bottles). **7.** Should be medium-size Dacron (Terylene). **8.** Consists of a length of steel strip, with one end made into a cutting edge by grinding. **9.** For this kind of scraper, it is preferable to have a soft iron blade which can be sharpened easily.

THE TOOLS OF CHAPTER 1

Legend:

1. Sailmaker's scissors. **2.** Hole-puncher. **3.** Orbital sander. **4.** Sailmaker's palm. **5.** Sailmaker's needles (most commonly used sizes: 14, 15, 16, 17, 18). **6.** Wooden needle-case. **7.** Waxed twine. **8/9.** Two different types of scraper.

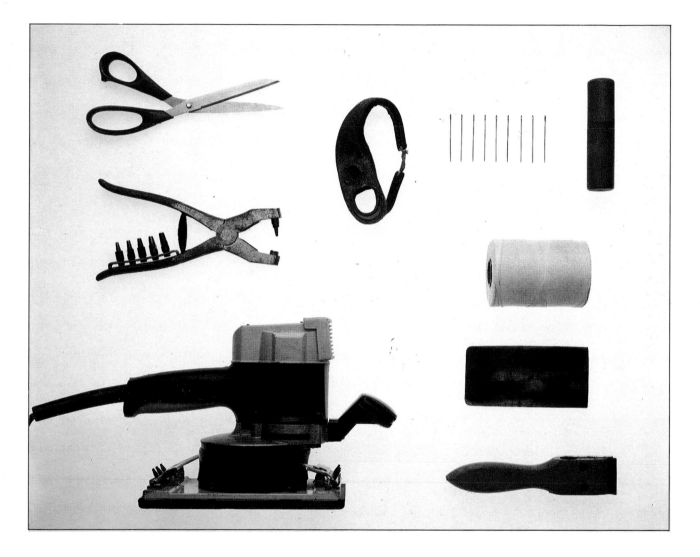

2. DECK FITTINGS

Planning the deck layout involves arranging the deck fittings of a sailing craft in direct relation to the intended use of the boat, to the type of rig and to the abilities of the crew who will be handling her.

As a rule, deck plans are carefully considered and worked out at the design stage; in the case of many mass-produced cruising boats, however, insufficient understanding of sailing problems combined with considerations of a purely economic nature often prevent an ideal solution being reached, and the deck fittings on the finished craft are not arranged for safe, easy, handy operation when working the sails. For this reason, the owner finds it necessary at times to introduce modifications and improvements himself.

WINCHES

Numerous manufacturers in several different countries produce winches. Leaders in the field include Lewmar, Barient, Barlow and Barbarossa.

Whatever the make of winch installed on your boat, regular periodic maintenance is a 'must' if you intend to get the full benefit from these invaluable aids to sail-handling. All winches should be given a major overhaul at least once a year.

New winches are delivered packed with a special type of extremely thick grease that is not suitable for marine use. For this reason, new winches must be dismantled completely and each component first cleaned very thoroughly with the help of a roll of paper towel, a soft brush and a basin full of solvent (petrol, paraffin, kerosene or even diesel oil), and then dried with a clean cloth. Before reassembling the winch, coat each part with a light film of lubricating oil (remember to use a clean brush). For years I have been using, with excellent results, a mixture made by adding approximately five per cent marine grease and five per cent STP engine oil additive to upper cylinder

Cutaway view of self-tailing winch showing bronze gears, spring-loaded pawls and roller bearings of central shaft.

lubricating oil (available from most motorcar spare parts dealers).

Before starting work, make sure that you have a copy of the maintenance manual for your particular type of winch; otherwise you run the risk of finding yourself with one or two components left over after reassembly! The tools required vary according to the type of winch. By the way, watch out when you handle the spring-loaded pawls; if not seated properly they tend to fly out all over the place. It is always advisable to keep a reserve stock of these components on board.

You should repeat the procedure described above each year, at the beginning of the sailing season, so as to rid your winch of any salt, grit or other dirt that may prevent the smooth operation of the gear mechanism.

Self-tailing winches

Winch versatility has been greatly increased by the introduction of the self-tailing system and the advantages gained fully justify the higher cost of the improved models.

Greater care must be taken, however, over the choice of ropes, since the jaws of the self-tailing system tend to accelerate rope wear (see Chapter 5).

Standard winches can be modified to self-tailing: for some makes this is only possible by replacing the entire drum assembly, but for others the operation is simpler and can be carried out with the help of a modification kit supplied on request by the manufacturers.

The self-tailing trip is normally positioned on the opposite side to where the rope enters the winch, as shown in the figure; in this way the rope can be hauled taut or slackened with greater ease.

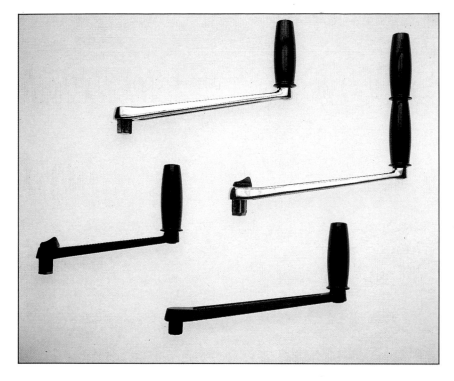

Light-alloy drums

It is a question of personal taste whether these drums are aesthetically more pleasing or not, but they certainly offer an appreciable saving in all-up weight. Their cost is usually not more than that of steel or chromium-plated bronze drums, but they can only be used for fibre rope.

Winch handles

It is advisable to have two-handed handles on winches for the genoa sheets as these permit the application of a far greater manual force. There are short handles too and jack handles for special uses. Handles fitted with safety catches are essential for winches installed on the mast or underneath the boom.

Light-alloy handles are more manageable, less dangerous and, consequently, well suited to medium-size and small boats as well as in general for work which does not require great manual force.

Handles, especially those fitted with safety catches, require periodic lubrication. Handles with handgrips mounted on roller bearings are also available.

From the top, proceeding clockwise: single-grip chromium-plated bronze handle without safety catch; double-grip chromium-plated bronze handle with safety catch; two single-grip light alloy handles, the first without and the second with safety catch. All four handles have grips mounted on roller bearings.
On opposite page: a range of light-alloy winches. The two on the left are standard two-speed models; the other two are self-tailing models. The table reproduced above serves as a guide for choosing the right type and size of winch. The numbers indicate the power ratio of the winch and are obtained by dividing the handle length by the drum diameter and multiplying the resulting quotient by the gear ratio.

| Approximate overall length (ft) | | | 19.5–25 | 25–27 | 30–32 | 33–35 | 35–36 | 36–39.5 | 39.5–41 |
		(metres)	6–7.60	7.60–8.25	9.10–9.75	10–10.70	10.70–11	11–12	12–12.50
SAIL AREA	Genoa	(sq. ft)	200	300	350	500	550	600	750
		(m²)	19	28	33	46	51	56	70
	Spinnaker	(sq. ft)	300	400	600	800	1000	1200	1400
		(m²)	28	37	56	74	93	111	130
	Mainsail	(sq. ft)	120	150	180	210	230	260	300
		(m²)	11	14	17	20	21	24	28
SHEETS	Genoa	Racing	8:1	16:1 or 24:1	30:1 or 40:1	43:1	46:1 or 48:1	48:1 or 55:1	55:1
		Cruising	7:1	16:1	30:1	40:1	43:1 or 46:1	46:1	46:1 or 48:1
	Spinnaker	Racing	6:1	8:1	16:1	30:1 or 40:1	40:1 or 43:1	43:1	46:1
		Cruising	6:1	7:1	8:1	16:1 or 24:1	30:1	30:1 or 40:1	40:1
	Mainsail	Racing		6:1	8:1	16:1	24:1	30:1	40:1
		Cruising		6:1	6:1	7:1	16:1	16:1	24:1
HALYARDS	Genoa	Racing	8:1	16:1	24:1	30:1 or 40:1	40:1 or 43:1	46:1	46:1
		Cruising	6:1	7:1	8:1 or 16:1	16:1 or 24:1	30:1	40:1 or 43:1	43:1
	Spinnaker	Racing	6:1	8:1	16:1	24:1 or 30:1	40:1	40:1 or 43:1	43:1
		Cruising	6:1	7:1	7:1	8:1	16:1	16:1 or 24:1	30:1
	Mainsail	Racing	6:1	7:1	8:1	16:1 or 24:1	30:1 or 40:1	40:1	40:1
		Cruising	6:1	6:1	7:1	8:1	16:1	24:1	30:1

SHEET TRACKS

Owing to deck space limitations, the mainsheet traveller track (even though the most important) is often positioned far from its ideal working position. Since it is difficult, if not impossible, in most cases to lengthen the track or change its position, the only thing you can do is to take steps to ensure its maximum efficiency. Naturally, the track must always be kept clean so that the car runs freely. Make sure that suitable rubber stops are fitted at each end of the track. It is also advisable to have athwartships purchases which will make it possible to move the car when it is heavily loaded. In addition, the car should be dismantled periodically, cleaned and greased to reduce friction to a minimum. The mainsheet blocks should be as far as possible coplanar in the vertical plane; if the mechanical advantage is too small, the number of falls can be increased by attaching an extra block to the boom (see Chapter 4).

The tracks serving the foresail sheets are frequently too short, or else have a section which in practice is never used; in this case, you can either add an extra length or cut off the surplus section and move it to another position where it will be more useful. For staysails or other special sails, an eye fastened to the deck is often sufficient for attaching the block or snatch-block for the sheet. It is of the utmost importance that the sheet has a clear run to the winch so as to avoid excessive friction and wear. A plastic terminal cap should be fitted to both ends of the track to prevent the car leaving it and also to protect your feet from the sharp edge of the track end. A moveable stop in the forward part of the genoa track, with a ring welded onto it, is often useful as an attachment point for blocks, snatch-blocks or luff tackle.

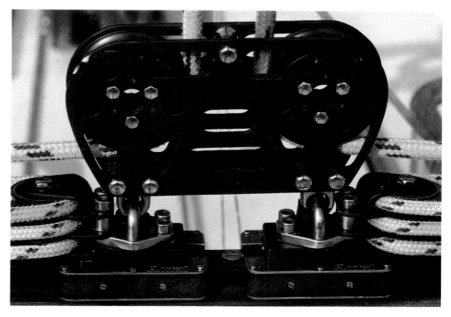

The photograph shows a double mainsheet block permitting the use of two winches.

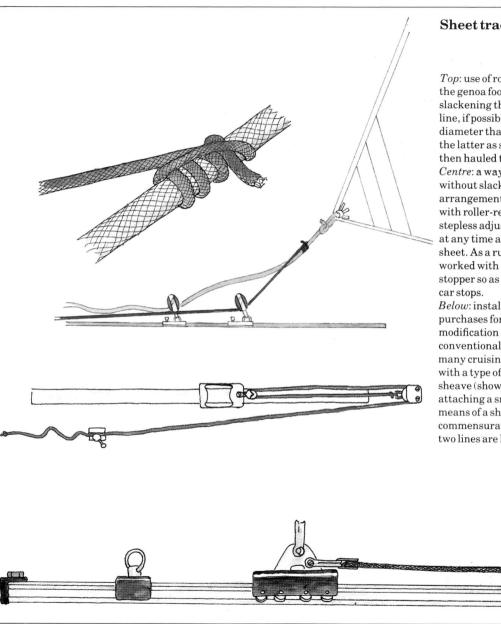

Sheet tracks

Top: use of rolling hitch in changing the genoa foot block position without slackening the sheet. A short length of line, if possible slightly smaller in diameter than the genoa sheet, is tied to the latter as shown in the detail and then hauled taut with a winch.
Centre: a way of shifting the genoa car without slackening the sheet. This arrangement is particularly effective with roller-reefing systems and permits stepless adjustment of the car position at any time and without slackening the sheet. As a rule, the control line is worked with a winch and made fast in a stopper so as to eliminate the need for car stops.
Below: installation of arthwartships purchases for mainsheet traveller. The modification consists in replacing the conventional end-stops installed in many cruising yachts (see left of sketch) with a type of end-stop that carries a sheave (shown on the right) and in attaching a small block to the car by means of a shackle of a size commensurate with the rope used. The two lines are held in jamming cleats.

Fixing leading blocks or other items of equipment to deck

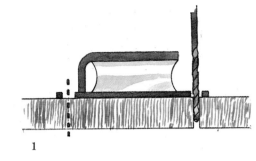

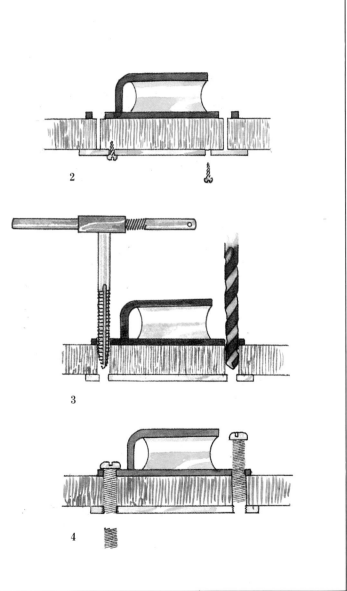

1. Once the item is positioned correctly on deck, drill pilot holes through planks (using a small-diameter bit) in such a way as to be able to establish the dimensions of the back-plate below deck. *2*. Fix back-plate in place with self-tapping screws, taking care that these do not coincide with the holes to be made for the bolts. *3*. From above, drill the required holes through deck and back-plate (for 6 mm diameter bolts, use 5 mm diameter bit). Using the appropriate tap wrench and screw tap, thread holes in back-plate. *4*. You can now screw in the bolts, smeared with sealing compound, and cut off the projecting ends of the bolts. Trim and finish off as required.

LEADING BLOCKS AND STOPPERS

The leading blocks for the genoa sheet deserve particular attention. On many boats they are often absent or, when installed, are not at the correct angle. Check the alignment with a piece of line and, if necessary, adjust the angle by inserting a wedge-shaped wooden shim between block and deck. Special types of leading block are available which incorporate stoppers and which make it easier to set and trim the genoa or spinnaker; watch out, though, for the control levers of the stoppers which project at deck level. Leading blocks are available in banks for taking halyards, topping lifts and other lines to the cockpit; they are usually combined with a bank of stoppers so that the various lines can all be handled by the same winch. The stoppers (or at least those for the halyards) should preferably be of the type that can be released even under load.

Leading blocks mounted on ball or roller bearings have become increasingly popular in recent years. If of good quality, they are well worth the extra cost since their efficiency is noticeably superior to that of conventional models. In addition, they are rugged, long-lasting and require only a minimum of maintenance.

Easy dismantling is an essential in both leading blocks and stoppers so that their component parts can be inspected and lubricated at regular intervals.

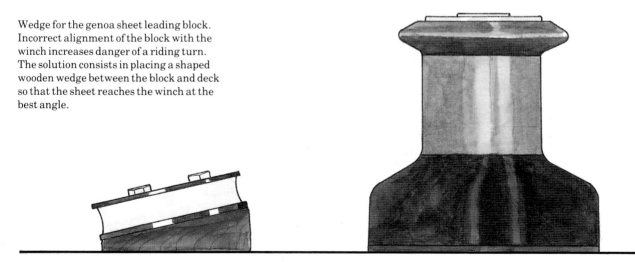

Wedge for the genoa sheet leading block. Incorrect alignment of the block with the winch increases danger of a riding turn. The solution consists in placing a shaped wooden wedge between the block and deck so that the sheet reaches the winch at the best angle.

RIGGING

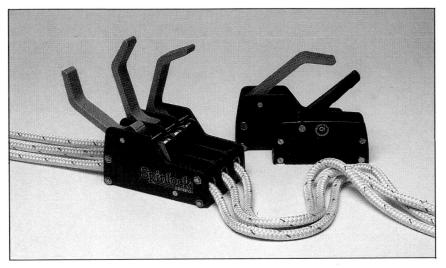

Above right: stoppers. On the left, a bank of three stoppers for ropes of up to 16 mm diameter; behind, two individual stoppers of different sizes.

Below: leading blocks. On the left, single and double-sheave genoa turning blocks, mounted on ball bearings; on the right, multiple halyard leading blocks for combining with a stopper bank (as shown in the photograph above left).

BLOCKS AND SNATCHBLOCKS

A deck accessory found on sailing vessels of the ancient world, the block has been continuously developed and improved over the years until today manufacturers offer a wide range to fit all needs. In fact the assortment is so great as to be almost bewildering; the important thing to remember is that the critical feature of a block is the quality of the material with which it is made, since failure of a block under load can have catastrophic results on board.

It is not always possible to find all the blocks you need in the range of one particular manufacturer. Take a look around at the lines of other manufacturers; the best solution often lies in combining blocks of different makes, each of which is just right for a particular purpose.

Blocks and snatchblocks. *From left to right*: *1*. single swivel block; *2*. swivel block with becket; *3*. fiddle block with becket; *4*. standing swivel block for fixing to deck; *5*. fiddle block with snap shackle; *6*. single block with snap shackle; *7*. snatchblock. *Uses*: *1*. spinnaker halyards; *2/3*. purchases; *4*. mainsheet; *5*. spinnaker sheet; *6*. spinnaker downhaul; *7*. spinnaker sheet/guy.

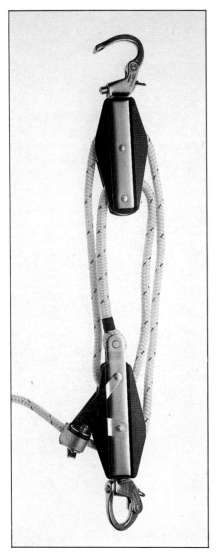

Block sizes must be chosen with care on the basis of the working loads involved, while the sheaves must have a groove profile appropriate to the type of rope served (wire or fibre). Blocks are now available fitted with a special mounting system which enables the block either to be left free to swivel around its vertical axis or to be fixed in one of two different positions at right angles to one another. Whenever possible, avoid using blocks fitted with jamming cleats since they are less versatile and more delicate than the ordinary type and, in addition, have a definite tendency to jam fast.

In my view, snatchblocks are an indispensable accessory. It is advisable to have a good many on board as they have many uses. Choose the type with soft rubber cheeks and a becket, which can be used for lashing the block with shock cord or a strop; fasten a lanyard to the ring of the snap shackle for easy quick release. A practical tip: when you wish to attach a snatchblock to a line under tension, make fast the snap shackle first and then open the block; slip it over the line and close with a sharp snap.

Always keep the sound components of old or damaged blocks and snatchblocks: you can use them as spare parts or, if you have enough, even reconstruct an entire new block.

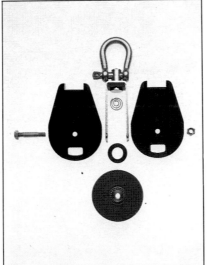

Left: exploded view of a block, showing the various component parts. Note sheave mounted on ball bearing and the mechanism permitting the block either to swivel freely or to be fixed in one or other of two positions at right angles to each other. *Far left*: multi-purpose luff tackle; an extremely practical accessory which should be kept always within reach.

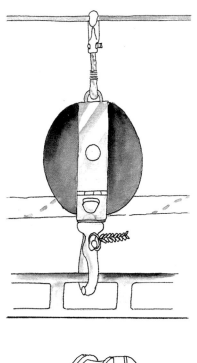

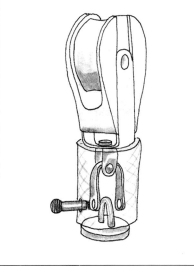

SPINNAKER GEAR

The particular characteristics of the spinnaker call for special equipment which must be kept in perfect order if we want to experience in full and in reasonable safety the thrills that this splendid sail can give on the high seas.

First of all, the spinnaker halyard block at the masthead should be rugged and of the swivel type. If the block is fastened by means of a shackle, see that the pin of the shackle is seized with two loops of Ormiston seizing wire and then fixed firmly with adhesive tape.

If a swivel has been attached to the spinnaker head, remove it: the

Above: snatchblock with becket fastened to shock cord. This arrangement is particularly useful in the case of spinnaker foot blocks, since it prevents the blocks from slamming against the deck when the boat is running before in light airs. *Below*: sleeve for holding blocks in an upright position. This highly practical device is easily made by cutting a length of robust armoured hose of appropriate diameter and punching a hole in its side for slipping home the shackle pin (very useful, for example, for leading blocks at the base of the mast).

swivel on a snap shackle does the job more efficiently and, in addition, is usually made of far tougher material.

The topping lift and downhaul must both be fastened as close as possible to the outboard end of the spinnaker boom. The downhaul foot block must be fitted centrally at the bows, in such a way that the downhaul can be worked efficiently on either tack without chafing against the pulpit or lifelines. If an eye has not been fitted to the deck for this particular block, you can either install one yourself or make the block fast to some nearby point (eg pulpit, rail or mooring cleat).

Both the topping lift and the downhaul should be led back to the cockpit and belayed near each other, so as to facilitate working the sail; in medium size and small boats, the down-haul can be handled without a winch but a reliable stopper is really the best solution for both ropes.

The spinnaker guy should be taken directly from the spinnaker boom to the winch, via a block or snatchblock fastened to the rail slightly forward of the beam. The sheet, on the other hand, is led from the clew to a fiddle block (ie a block with two sheaves of different diameters, one above the other) fastened to the aft end of the rail. When the spinnaker has to be squared up, control can be improved by leading the sheet through a snatchblock attached to the rail more or less at the same point as the snatchblock for the guy on the opposite rail. If you have been farsighted and fastened a snatchblock on each side, just forward of the beam, they can be used alternately for the guy and for the sheet.

A WORD TO THE WISE

Boat shows are the best places for picking up the catalogues of nautical equipment manufacturers. Collect as many as you can and look them over at leisure at home, comparing the various makes before coming to a final decision.

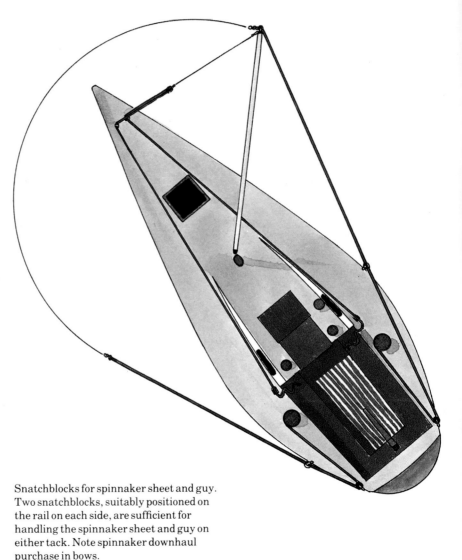

Snatchblocks for spinnaker sheet and guy. Two snatchblocks, suitably positioned on the rail on each side, are sufficient for handling the spinnaker sheet and guy on either tack. Note spinnaker downhaul purchase in bows.

THE TOOLS OF CHAPTER 2

With the exception of the sailmaker's palm, waxed twine, sailmaker's needles and shock cord, the tools are the same as those listed and illustrated in Chapter 4, ie screw taps, tap wrench, screwdriver, stainless steel folding rule, electric drill with high-speed bits. To these you should add a bastard file, a toolmaker's file and a set of Allen keys (the type below solves the eternal problem of the missing size of this tool).

Above: foot blocks for spinnaker downhaul. If an eye has not been fitted on deck in the bows, the block can be lashed to the rail with a strop (tubular webbing is best) as shown in the figure. If the rail on your boat stops short of the bows you can use the mooring cleats.
Below, left: fiddle block. Permits switching from the normal heavy sheet to a light sheet when the wind drops.

Below, right: fastening of spinnaker masthead block. The block, of the swivel type, is generally shackled to a U-bolt pad. The U-bolt must have castle nuts, locked with split pins. The shackle pin making fast the block must be secured with several turns of seizing wire (Ormiston) and protected by adhesive tape.

3. THE MAST

In a certain sense, the mast can be regarded as the life force of a sailing boat: take away the mast and the craft immediately becomes nothing more than a floating platform. Aim at getting to know your mast well and take the greatest possible care of it, since it plays a fundamental part in the propulsive system of your boat.

Masts can be stepped either on the deck or on the keel. Deck-stepped masts are usually suitable for small-to-medium boats: that is, up to a maximum overall length of 33–36 ft (10–11 m). Beyond these dimensions, a deck-stepped mast is acceptable only in a few special cases.

In fact, it must not be forgotten that the compression force applied to the mast step by the mast can reach levels as high as one and a half to two times the displacement of the boat.

MAST TRIM

Before going into this subject in detail, I think it is important to stress some basic requirements of a mast with just one set of spreaders. Chain plates and all other connections for shrouds or stays must be able to withstand a load approximately equal to the displacement of the boat. The anchorage for the upper shroud should be located centrally on the side of the mast; it can be shifted, if necessary, up to ¾ in (20 mm) towards the stern but never towards the bows. The angle formed by the forward lower shroud and the mast should be at least five degrees; in the case of the aft lower shroud, on the other hand, the angle can be reduced to three degrees. The terminals of stays and shrouds must be fitted with toggles and pins so that they will adjust to the angle of the stay or shroud. The forward and after edges of the mast heel should be slightly rounded so as to spread the load evenly on the mast step when the mast bends.

If your boat has a keel-stepped mast, you will need to install suitable rubber shims to ensure that the mast is wedged firmly into the mast partners. Solid, hard rubber

wedges cut to length are used for this purpose. The wedges are inserted fore and aft only, so that there is the possibility of a slight lateral movement on the part of the mast to compensate for the inevitable stretching of the shrouds. Wedging is generally carried out below deck, after slackening the standing rigging and setting up a luff tackle for shifting the mast in the fore-and-aft plane.

You can now turn your attention to adjusting the trim of the mast, first lowering the boom onto the deck and checking that all lifts and halyards are slack. In addition, remove the mainsail which at this stage can be a nuisance.

First of all, check that the mast is vertical and well centred both fore-and-aft and athwartships. To do this, tighten the forestay, backstay and upper shrouds (without applying too much tension) and then sight mast from a point on the shore sufficiently far from the boat, using for comparison a shore structure with a perfectly vertical profile (eg a lamppost or the corner of a building).

Tighten the upper shrouds to a tension approximately equal to ten per cent of the displacement of the boat and then proceed to tighten the lower shrouds, checking at in-

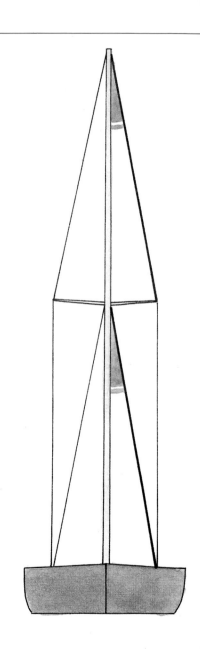

Shroud angles

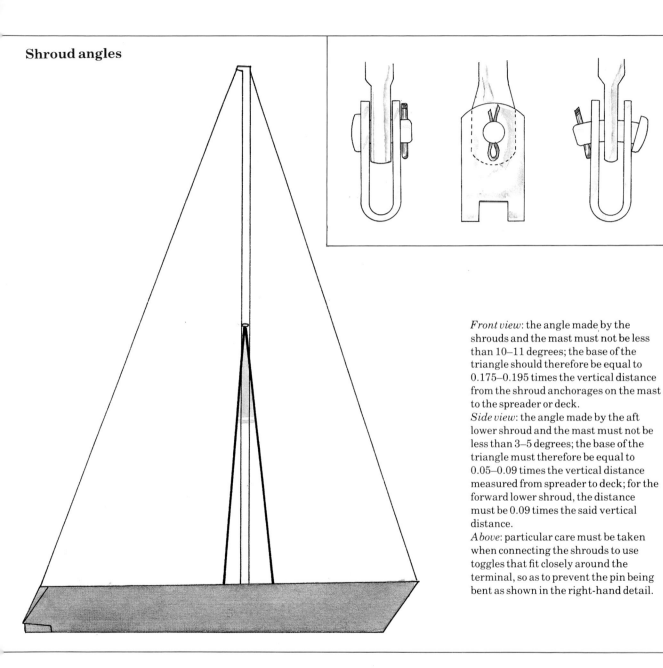

Front view: the angle made by the shrouds and the mast must not be less than 10–11 degrees; the base of the triangle should therefore be equal to 0.175–0.195 times the vertical distance from the shroud anchorages on the mast to the spreader or deck.

Side view: the angle made by the aft lower shroud and the mast must not be less than 3–5 degrees; the base of the triangle must therefore be equal to 0.05–0.09 times the vertical distance measured from spreader to deck; for the forward lower shroud, the distance must be 0.09 times the said vertical distance.

Above: particular care must be taken when connecting the shrouds to use toggles that fit closely around the terminal, so as to prevent the pin being bent as shown in the right-hand detail.

Mast trim

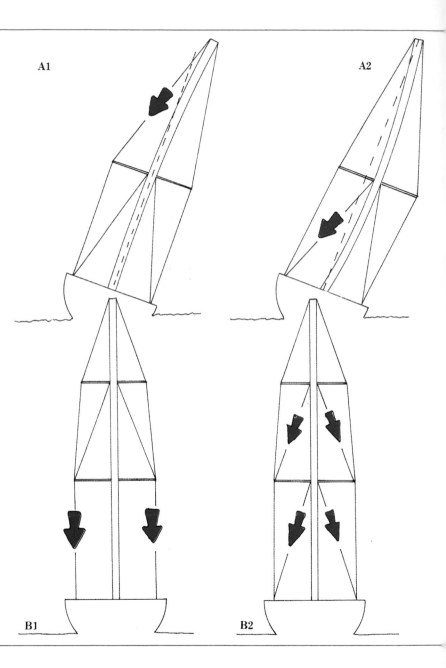

A1

A2

B1

B2

The correct sequence for setting up the standing rigging of a mast with a double spreader rig is illustrated in drawings *B1* and *B2*. After checking that the mast is properly centred both fore-and-aft and athwartships, start by tightening the two upper shrouds and check, with a steel folding rule, the distance between their end terminals and the deck. Now tighten first the intermediate shrouds and then the lower shrouds. After this preliminary trimming, final adjustments should be carried out at sea; sailing close to the wind under full sail and with the boat heeling at least 15 degrees, check that the mast is straight by sighting along the mast track. Figures *B3*, *B4* and *B5* show schematically the rigging adjustments required for trueing the mast to the vertical in three different cases of irregular curvature; in each case the mast should end up as close as possible to the true vertical on both tacks. Figures *A1–A5* schematize five different situations which can arise with a mast with one set of spreaders, together with the necessary rigging adjustments.

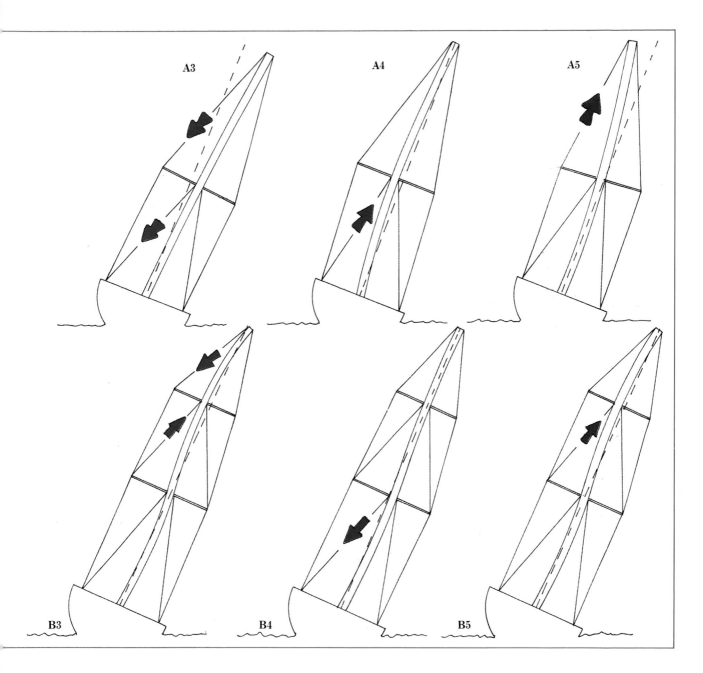

RIGGING

tervals by sighting along the mast track. Tighten the forward lower shrouds first, and the babystay too (if present), until the mast is raked slightly aft at the height of the spreaders; then tighten the aft lower shrouds. Final adjustment of the mast trim is carried out at sea, sailing close-hauled and under full sail with the boat heeling at least 15 degrees.

The mast track alignment will provide confirmation as to whether the mast is or is not vertical; the track should not deviate from the vertical by more than one per cent of the mast height.

It is also important to check that the spreaders are positioned correctly. Ideally, the spreader should bisect the angle formed by the shroud across its end. For this reason, spreaders are always angled slightly upwards since, in this way, the compression load applied by the shroud to the windward spreader is distributed linearly along it; otherwise there is a definite risk of bending the spreader or snapping the connection to the mast – and even of denting the mast itself.

Once you have completed all adjustments to the mast trim, insert split pins in all turnbuckles and finish off by protecting them

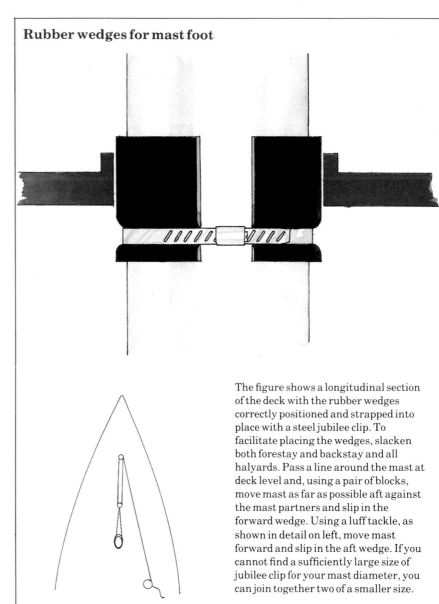

Rubber wedges for mast foot

The figure shows a longitudinal section of the deck with the rubber wedges correctly positioned and strapped into place with a steel jubilee clip. To facilitate placing the wedges, slacken both forestay and backstay and all halyards. Pass a line around the mast at deck level and, using a pair of blocks, move mast as far as possible aft against the mast partners and slip in the forward wedge. Using a luff tackle, as shown in detail on left, move mast forward and slip in the aft wedge. If you cannot find a sufficiently large size of jubilee clip for your mast diameter, you can join together two of a smaller size.

with a wrapping of adhesive tape.

Many will have noticed the increasing use during the last few years of a special silver-grey linenized tape, especially on racing yachts. Called 'duct tape' and originating in the United States (where it is used by plumbers for sealing waterpipes), it is tough, strongly adhesive and damp-proof, qualities which make it particularly well suited for use on all standing and running rigging. Duct tape is still rather an expensive product, but its higher cost is fully justified by the thousand and one uses to which it can be put on board.

STANDING RIGGING

Rod or wire rigging? Stainless steel rod has a stretch coefficient that is 20 per cent less than that of a 1 × 19 stainless steel wire of equal diameter. Compared to wire rigging, however, rod rigging is less flexible, more difficult to install and adjust, more costly and its average useful life (under normal conditions) is around two years. Beyond this period, rod rigging is apt to become unreliable owing to metal fatigue, a condition which cannot be detected by the naked eye or even, at times, with

the aid of sophisticated instruments. All things considered, then, this type of rigging is not recommended for ordinary pleasure cruisers for which the standard 1 × 19 stainless steel wire is far more suitable.

It is extremely useful to be able to measure the amount of tension in a stay or shroud after tensioning operations have been completed and special instruments are now available on the market for doing this. If you do not have this equipment, you can use this formula for stress values which do not exceed 50 per cent of the ultimate strength of the wire:

$$\text{Tension} = (\text{overall elongation} \times \\ \text{breaking load} \times 100) \\ \div \text{ overall length of} \\ \text{rope}$$

To apply the formula, first take up the slack in the stay without, however, stretching it; measure accurately and mark off (with a felt pen or with pieces of adhesive tape) a reference length, preferably in the central section of the stay. Then tension the stay as required and measure the elongation of the reference length.

To simplify the calculation, a factor of the overall length of the

rope is usually adopted as reference length. For example, if your stay is 30 ft (10 m) long, measure off 6 ft (2 m) as a reference length; the overall elongation of the whole rope will be five times the elongation of the reference length.

For safety the tension of a given stay or shroud should not exceed 25 per cent of its ultimate strength rating, although there is no danger of failure for stresses of up to 50 per cent of the nominal breaking load.

These checks come in very handy if it is necessary to apply a heavy load to the standing rigging when adjusting the mast, since they indicate when it would be advisable to substitute larger-diameter wire.

The final adjustment of the shrouds should not be carried out while the boat is at her berth, since the loads involved are generally high and there is a definite risk of damaging the turnbuckle threads. It is better to put to sea and finish the job while under sail on a reach, taking advantage of the slackness of the leeward shrouds on each tack.

There are various types of terminal for 1 × 19 semi-flexible wire stays. The most common type is the swaged socket, with eye or fork attachment; there are also terminals that can be fastened to the wire rope by hand, without the help of special tools, ranging from the traditional Norseman type to the revolutionary Douglas and Sta-lok models. Keep a reserve stock of the most commonly used sizes of these terminals on board so as to be ready for any emergency. If they are Norseman terminals, remember (a) to fill them up with sealing compound to prevent the seawater seeping in and accelerating the processes of corrosion and (b) to smear the threads with Loctite to ensure a secure fit of the screw-in part.

The 7 × 19 strand flexible wire ropes, used for running rigging, can be terminated with an eye spliced by hand or secured by a Talurit or Nicopress splice (special copper or steel sleeves which are slipped onto the rope and then

On opposite page: some types of stainless steel wire ropes (breaking loads and weights are given in the accompanying table). From left to right: *1.* 1 × 19 wire rope for standing rigging; *2.* as item 1 but of smaller diameter; *3.* 7 × 7 (49-strand) semi-flexible wire for lifelines and sundry uses; *4.* 7 × 19 (133-strand) flexible wire for running rigging (halyards, topping lift, strops, etc).

Construction	Diameter (mm)	Unit Weight (lb/ft)	(kg/hm)	Breaking Load (lb)	(kg)
1 × 19	2	0.014	2.02	785	355
	2.5	0.023	3.42	1200	545
	3	0.031	4.55	1730	785
	4	0.054	8.09	3065	1390
	5	0.085	12.65	4800	2178
	6	0.122	18.19	6735	3055
	7	0.166	24.72	8985	4075
	8	0.218	32.37	11550	5240
	10	0.339	50.47	17705	8030
	12	0.489	72.7	24140	10950
	14	0.665	99	32410	14700
	16	0.874	130	41780	18950
	18	1.078	160.5	51700	23450
	20	1.357	201.88	62720	28450
	22	1.641	244.27	73305	33250
7 × 7	2	0.011	1.65	550	250
	2.5	0.017	2.6	840	380
	3	0.025	3.7	1235	560
	4	0.044	6.56	2205	1000
	5	0.069	10.24	3420	1550
	6	0.099	14.8	4960	2250
	7	0.135	20.11	6725	3050
	8	0.176	26.25	8820	4000
	10	0.272	40.45	13560	6150
7 × 19	2.5	0.018	2.64	840	380
	3	0.025	3.78	1215	550
	4	0.043	6.4	2030	920
	5	0.069	10.31	3265	1480
	6	0.102	15.14	4805	2180
	7	0.135	20.03	6395	2900
	8	0.179	26.58	8380	3800
	10	0.277	41.23	13115	5950

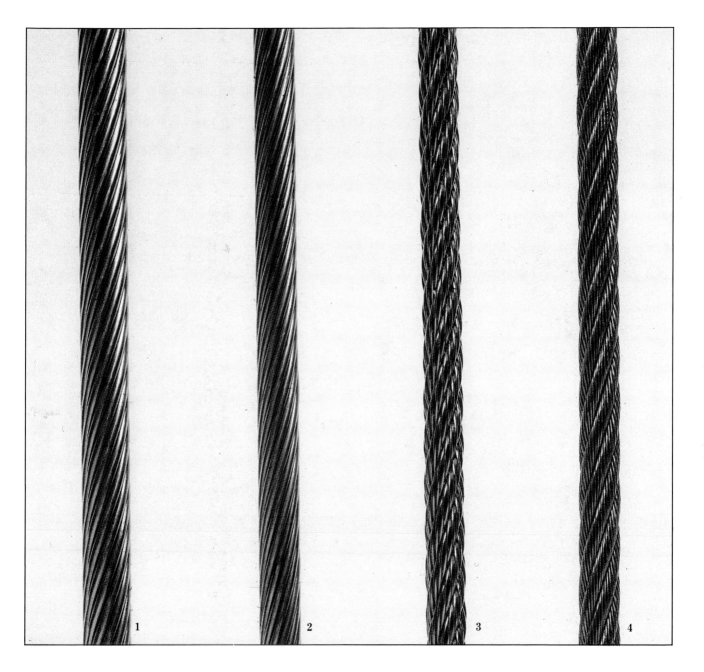

1   2   3   4

squeezed tight, either by hand using a special swage or by machine with a hydraulic press).

During periodic routine inspections of the rigging, special attention should be paid to the forestay which is possibly the most severely stressed of all the standing rigging. In addition to bearing the full thrust of the foresails, the stay is subject to the vibrations from the flapping of the jibs and, above all, to fatigue stress when, in a choppy head sea, the repeated slamming of the boat against the waves and the resultant bending and unbending of the hull is accompanied by alternate sudden slackening and violent tautening of the stay.

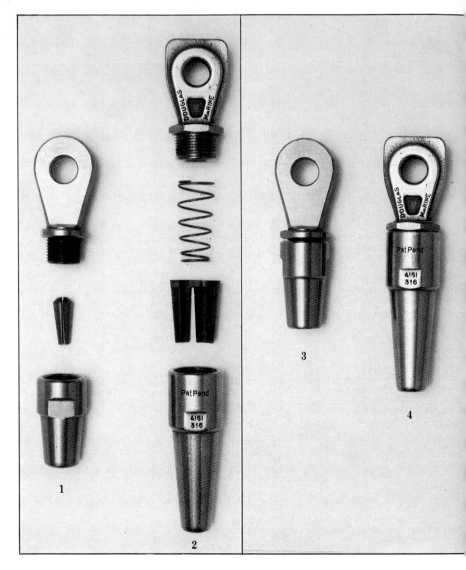

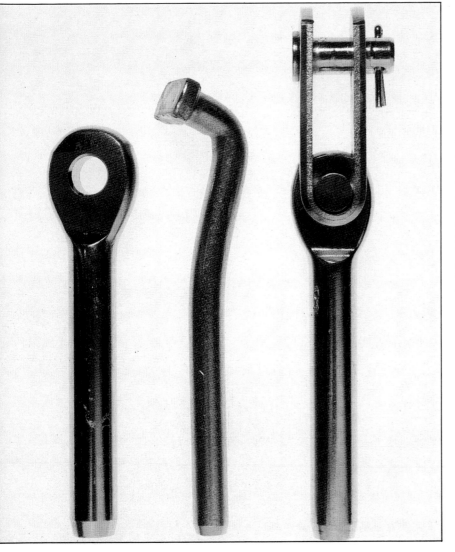

On left: clamp-on shroud terminals. From left to right: eye terminal, T ball terminal, toggle terminal.

On opposite page: 1. & 3. Norseman eye terminal for 1 × 19 or 7 × 7 wire ropes. This classic and well-known stay terminal requires no comment; grip on the cable is provided by interchangeable internal clamping cones which match the wire type (1 × 19 or 7 × 7). Fitting Norseman terminals requires a certain dexterity and the work must be carried out accurately to ensure a firm grip. *2. & 4.* Douglas terminal. These revolutionary terminals operate on the principle of the Morse taper and can be used for any type of rigging, from rod to 7 × 19 wire rope. Precision-cast in AISI 316 stainless steel, Douglas terminals are entirely self-adjusting and are fitted in no time: simply loosen the cap, thread in the end of the shroud and tighten the cap again.

51

Masthead equipment

From left to right (forward to aft): wind direction and airspeed sensors, tri-colour masthead light, radar reflector, Windex.

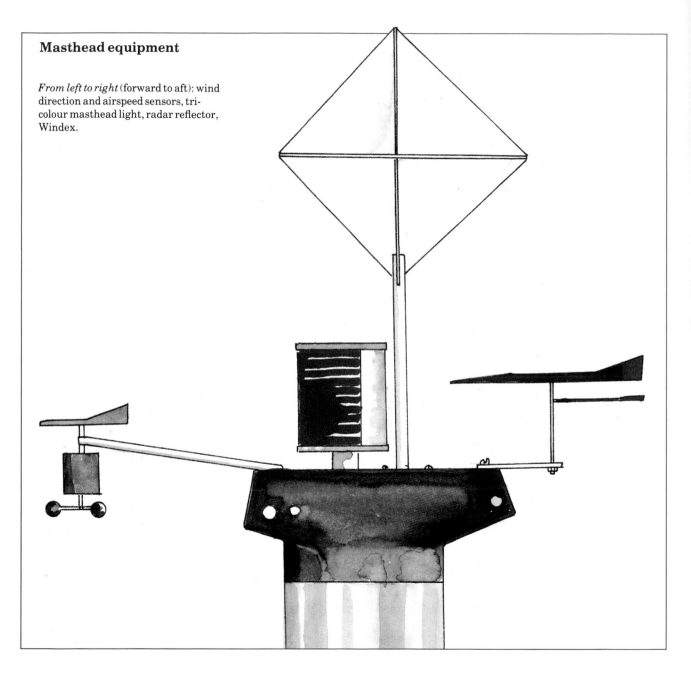

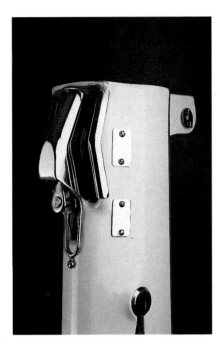

Masthead details. The central guard protects the forestay connection and, at the same time, prevents the two halyards on either side from chafing against the stay. The exit for the central third halyard, normally used for the genoa, is visible beneath the guard. The two small plates fastened with screws permit easy removal of the sheaves for inspection.

THE MASTHEAD

This highly important part of the mast must be inspected thoroughly at regular intervals.

Provide yourself with a good make of bosun's chair and find a competent person to assist you from the deck. A piece of advice: never trust the snap shackles on topping lifts and halyards, but fasten the bosun's chair directly to the eye splice by means of a shackle or with several turns of strong rope or tubular webbing. Another good tip: tie all the tools you are taking aloft either to yourself or to the chair, with long enough lengths of line for you to be able to work in peace of mind and without running the risk of dropping anything onto the deck, with consequences that are easily imaginable.

Once aloft, carry out the following inspections: check the connections of upper shrouds and stays for signs of wear (ovalization of eye, bent shackle pins); look for cracks in the corners of sheave slots; check that sheaves revolve freely and that the grooves are smooth and free from cracks or indentations which might damage halyards; check fastenings of all equipment installed at the masthead (lights, wind instruments, aerials); see that all nuts are split-pinned with the pin ends bent well back. If you have to replace a topping lift or halyard, use a small-size messenger line with a short length of chain or a shackle pin attached as a weight.

If the masthead needs extensive repairs, you will find it more practical to remove the mast and carry out the work on land. In any case, the mast should be unstepped for a major overhaul at least once every two or three years. This could be a good opportunity for adding a couple of useful gadgets to the masthead gear: (i) a tri-colour masthead light which, given its high degree of visibility, contributes considerably to your safety at sea; (ii) a Windex, that very simple and practical instrument consisting of two sights and a revolving pointer which indicates the apparent wind direction.

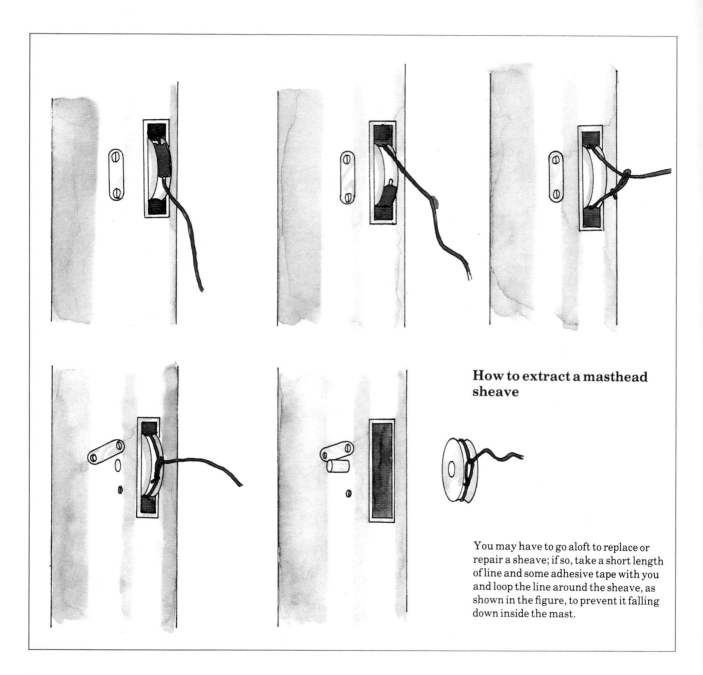

How to extract a masthead sheave

You may have to go aloft to replace or repair a sheave; if so, take a short length of line and some adhesive tape with you and loop the line around the sheave, as shown in the figure, to prevent it falling down inside the mast.

SPREADERS

There are two main types of spreader: round- or wing-shaped. The first can withstand compression loads only and is generally fitted on masts which have double lower shrouds. The wing-shaped type on the other hand, can also withstand heavy bending loads in the fore-and-aft plane and for this reason is adopted for flexible masts.

Under certain wind conditions, the mast is subjected to severe bending in order to flatten the mainsail; as a result, the connection of the spreader to the mast is stressed to a very high degree and, if the fastening arrangement is not sufficiently strong or is incorrectly designed, serious problems can arise including the possibility of dismasting. Although such problems concern the out-and-out racing man more than the ordinary cruising yachtsman, I have chosen to mention them because only too often one sees, in every marina, boats with spreaders in a dangerously bad state of repair. Never forget that if the spreaders collapse unexpectedly, the chances are that your mast will go too!

Check the spreader connections on every possible occasion to see that they present no visible signs of fatigue, that there are no dents in the mast wall in their proximity and that all the components fit properly without too much play. If you have any doubts, call in an expert.

Recommended measures are (a) binding the spreaders to prevent wear from the continual chafing of halyards and runners, and (b) padding the tips of the crosstrees so that they cannot hole the genoa when going about.

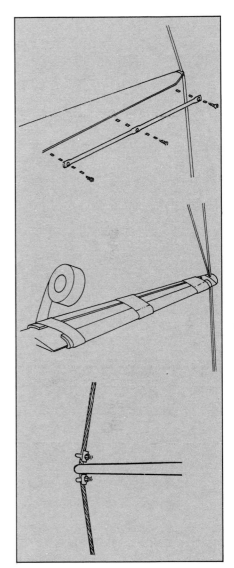

Two systems for protecting crosstrees from wear due to the chafing of halyards and runners. The first system (*top*) consists in screwing a small stainless steel pipe to the edge of the spreader; the second system (*centre*) uses the two halves of a piece of reinforced plastic pipe split longitudinally, slipped onto the spreader and held in place by adhesive tape. *Below*: fixing the spreader to the shroud. To ensure that the two angles are the same, the spreader tip must be held slightly above the horizontal. This can be done by using two C-clamps as shown in the figure.

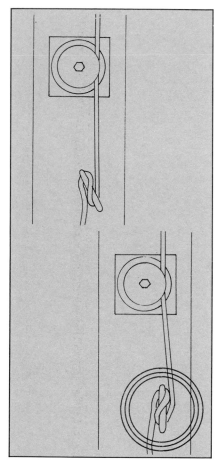

Mast cleats should be positioned as shown top left, ie tilted slightly from the vertical so as to facilitate making fast the halyard.

HOW TO GET THE BEST FROM YOUR MAST

Halyard exits

Several different systems are now available, but the double-sheave arrangement is still the most effective since it prevents wear both of the mast wall and of the halyard. In this case, the correct alignment of the halyard exit with the leading block at the foot of the mast is essential.

Winch base-plates

Most winches have bronze base-plates which, when they come into contact with light alloy surfaces, can give rise to galvanic corrosion problems. Where the winch is mounted on an alloy mast, therefore, it is advisable to insert a layer of insulating material (tufnol, nylon, wood) between mast and base-plate.

Rivets or screws?

The majority of boatbuilders use rivets for fastening the mast fittings. Rivets are an extremely practical type of fastening, but in this particular case have two serious limitations: first, they are not as strong as a screw of equal diameter and, secondly, they can only be removed by shearing them off.

If rivets are used, they should be always of monel (a nickel-copper alloy) and the hole should be filled with sealing compound before the rivet is inserted and hammered home. The use of rivets should be limited to fastening items which are not subject to heavy loads and, in any case, only to small to medium-size boats of 20–30 ft (6–9 m).

Drilling and threading a hole in a light alloy structure is a comparatively simple operation that almost anyone can manage satisfactorily. Stainless steel screws should be used, smeared with something that will prevent galvanic action from jamming the screw in its aluminium seating: white lead can be used or a drop of paint or, as an alternative, silicone. If you have to dismantle the mast for major repairs, you can take the opportunity to treat all the screws of the mast in this way; it is without doubt a long and tedious job, but one which in the long run will probably pay off by saving you much trouble while sailing.

Split pins, nuts, bolts

It is advisable to use only stainless steel split pins and to bend them back at least 15–20 degrees. Bolts should fit snugly and be of the right length. Through-bolts should have lock-nuts (or, better still, split-pinned nuts) to prevent accidental loosening. Nuts and split pins should be coated with a little silicone to prevent damage to sails or rigging. If possible, avoid using split rings: apart from being bulkier, these rings are weak, ductile and easily dislodged by nearby running rigging.

Shape of mast heel. The heel of the mast should be chamfered on the forward and aft edges to ensure an even distribution of the load in all situations. This is particularly important in the case of masts subjected to severe bending forces.

Mast track

The mast track must be kept scrupulously clean so that the slides attached to the mainsail can travel up and down the track smoothly and without jamming.

Make sure that the foot latch works efficiently and will not jam the slides during reefing. Lubricate slides from time to time with a Teflon spray or with a little vaseline.

Many mainsails, particularly on small boats, have slides secured by shackles. This system, however, often causes the mainsail to stick halfway up the mast owing to misalignment of the shackles; in addition, shackles are noisy and, rattling against the mast, often end up by ruining the surface. It is far better to fix the slides to the sail by means of hanks made of several turns of tubular webbing sewn together.

The four drawings show the sequence of operations for sewing on mainsail hanks; use tubular tape, extra-strong waxed twine and size 15/16 sail needles.

Mast coat

Tyre inner tube is the ideal material for the mast inner coat, since it is already the right shape. Cut to length and fix over mast partners with jubilee clips first at the top, then the bottom. Seal both upper and lower joins with silicone. The outer canvas cover has a purely decorative function and is secured in place with Velcro strips or with a draw-string.

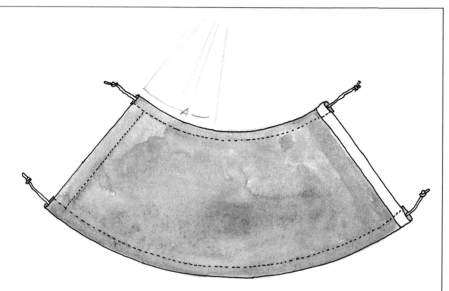

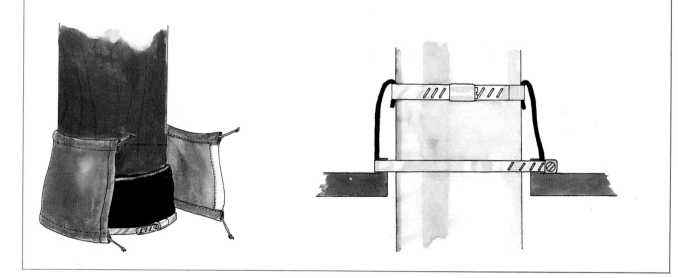

Runner and lever shrouds

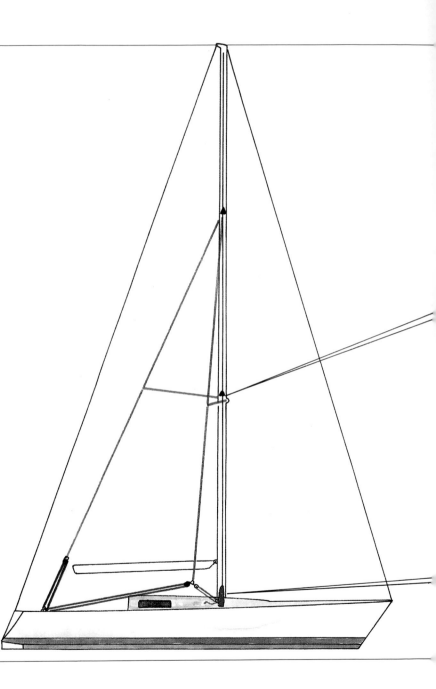

Anyone who has a mast fitted with two sets of spreaders and runners will certainly have had the exasperating experience of having the slack leeside runner swinging constantly to and fro. A practical way to eliminate this annoyance is to reeve a length of shock cord through an eye on the fore side of the mast and make the ends fast to the two stays. The leeward stay is automatically hauled close to the mast when the stay on the windward side is hauled taut, and vice versa. The lower end of the stay can be lashed by means of a tackle made fast to the chain plate with a strop or shackle. The inset shows the knot for making shock cord fast to the stays.

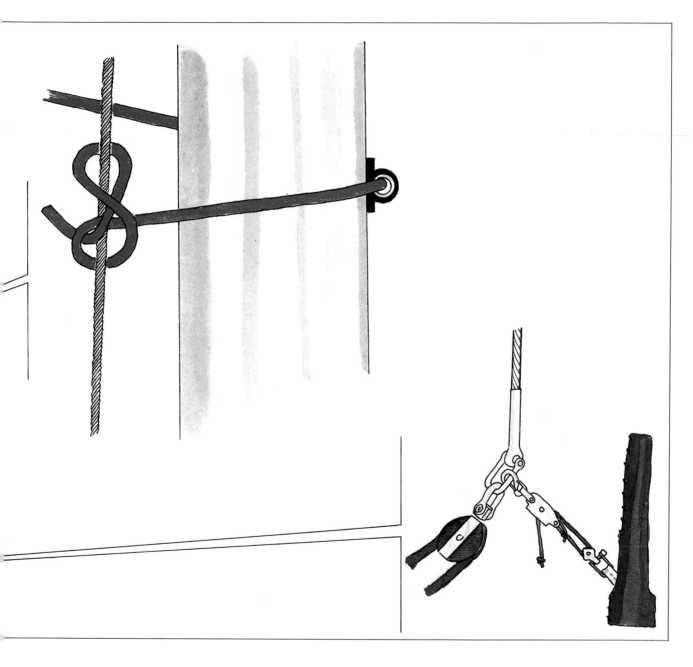

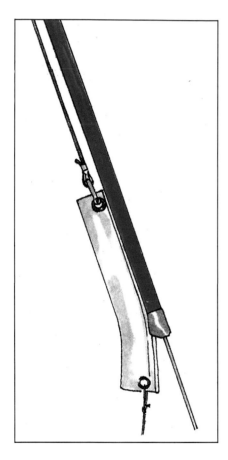

Use a length of tape of suitable size, fitted with two eyelets, for cleaning the groove. Thread edge of tape into track, attach a halyard onto the upper eyelet and a suitable line to the lower one, and slide tape up and down the track. Teflon spray is a good lubricant for the job.

ROLLER-REEFER SYSTEMS

Roller-reefer systems have been installed on an increasing number of boats during the past few years, both for the mainsail and for the headsails. These systems simplify considerably the business of working the sails on cruising craft and encourage even the laziest yachtsman to hoist his sails more often.

Mainsail roller-reefer systems are a fairly recent development and, as such, their operation is not yet entirely trouble-free. The vertical type, which furls the mainsail inside the mast, presents some problems, above all in connection with the length of the worm screw (which is, in fact, as long as the mast); in addition, if the mechanism does jam there is less possibility of a jury rig. The horizontal type which furls the mainsail inside the boom is, in my opinion, preferable for two reasons: in the first place, if the mechanism fails,

From left to right: three types of mainsail: conventional, roller-reefer, horizontal roller-reefer.

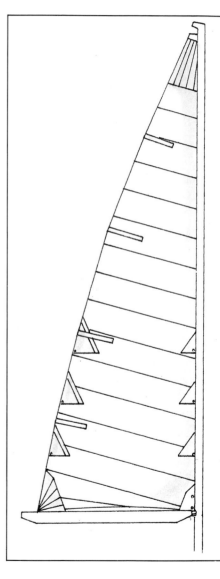

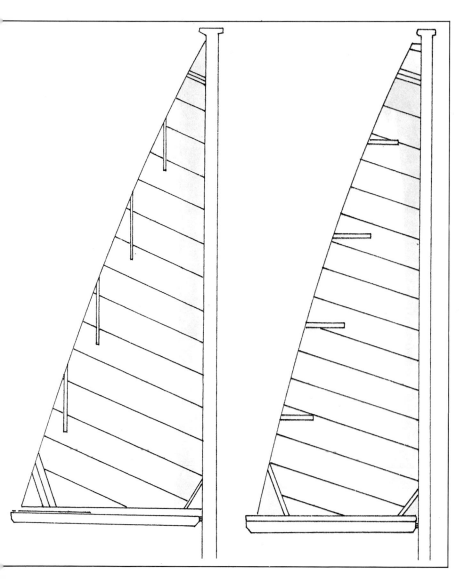

it is always possible to lower and reef the sail in the usual way; secondly, no substantial modification of the mast is required.

Viewed impartially, however, the practical utility of these systems seems rather doubtful given the many advantages offered by the traditional mainsail.

Headsail roller-reefer systems, on the other hand, are quite another matter. By now they have stood the test of several years' active service and, as a result, offer a reasonable guarantee of reliable and easy operation. A great variety of models can be found on the market, ranging from the simple manual roller to sophisticated hydraulic systems. The only difficulty is in choosing!

Good, reliable operation of roller-reefer systems depends above all on the proper upkeep and use of certain pieces of equipment. First of all, the groove in the foil must always be kept clean and well-lubricated (a Teflon spray is suitable) so that the sail will not jam in the groove. Secondly, if the stay is sectional, dismantle it periodically and check whether the ends of the extruded sections have suffered any damage or deformation which might pinch or tear the sail. Finally, the halyard must always be

Roller-reefer systems

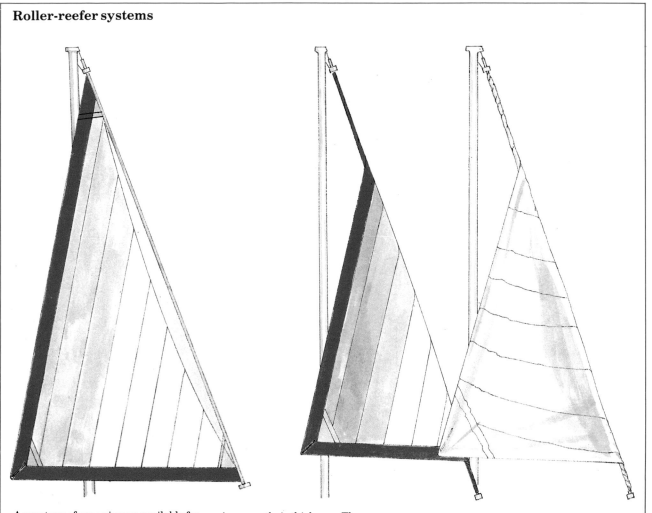

A new type of genoa is now available for use with roller-reefer systems with vertically-cut panels of different cloth; the foot and the leech have borders padded with synthetic material which increase their thickness. These modifications ensure that, unlike the traditional genoa, the sail will not crease or ruck when partially rolled up.

hoisted to the top of the foil; sails having a luff shorter than the foil must be attached to the top roller by means of a span of suitable length, otherwise the end of the halyard will get twisted around the foil causing extensive damage.

Another component part to be checked as often as possible is the feeder; this controls the alignment of the luff-rope as it enters the grooved foil and allows the sail to slide smoothly up the foil. A pre-feeder is generally lashed to the stay slightly below the feeder to ensure a perfect alignment of the luff-rope during hoisting.

The furling drum should be rinsed frequently with fresh water to eliminate salt deposits; a drop of oil from time to time will also do no harm, even though (in theory) the drum is self-lubricating. The control line must be aligned correctly so that it will work efficiently; you can also submit the line to a slimming process to reduce the volume of the coils on the drum. Wire, in my opinion, is not required in this case; use instead a good-quality fibre rope that will last a long time and give you no problems.

To conclude, take good care of your mast and of all its fittings: the safety and performance of your boat are to a great extent

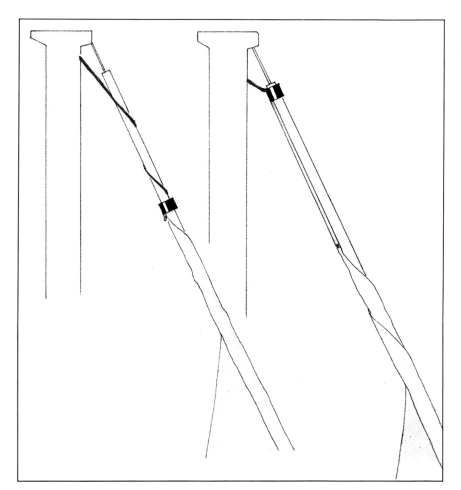

A useful gadget for headsail roller-reefer systems. Sails which have a luff shorter than the foil must be attached to the upper roller by means of a wire strop of suitable length; the strops are sheathed with tape or plastic and made fast to the head. This precaution prevents the halyard from twisting around the forestay when the sail is furled.

RIGGING

dependent on their efficiency. If you can, unstep the mast every two or three years and bring it ashore for a thorough check and service of all its components. Don't give way to laziness during the sailing season either: get into the bosun's chair and go aloft to check that everything is in good order – at least you will be rewarded with a better view from the masthead!

If you have to unstep the mast for maintenance, or for any other reason, it is advisable first to remove the roller-reefer foil; this can be done with the aid of a halyard and some helpers, taking care to lower the foil without bending it excessively to avoid damaging the connections between the extruded sections, or kinking.

An ideal sail plan for a cruising boat with roller-reefer headsail is shown in the figure alongside. The aero-dynamic efficiency is adequate even when the cut of the headsails is not perfect. When sailing close-hauled in a fresh breeze, however, it is necessary to change the jib instead of rolling it up on the stay.

Ideal cruising rig

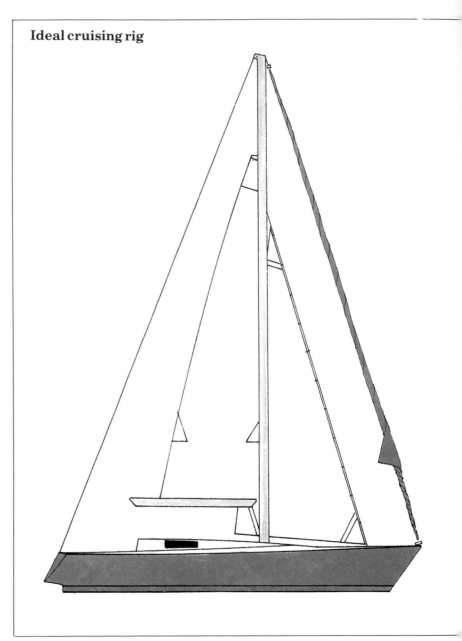

1. A good solution for the cruising yachtsman is this combination of a medium–large roller-reefer genoa with a staysail (possibly fitted with one row of reef points) bent to the babystay.

2. When it is necessary to shorten sail rapidly, it is sufficient to take in one reef of the mainsail, roll up the jib and hoist the staysail kept ready for immediate use at the foot of the babystay. In this way a more balanced sail plan is obtained, with the centre of effort shifted slightly aft and, consequently, a reduced tendency for the bows to bury in the waves. In addition, a pronounced slot effect is maintained with improved performance when sailing close-hauled.

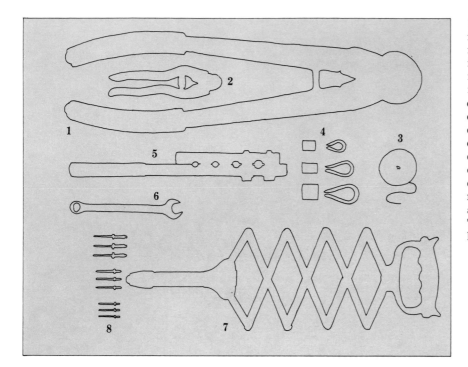

1/2. Felco have cornered the market in this field for many years. Their shears are reliable, strong and practically indestructible. **3.** Ormiston wire is made of monel and is invaluable on board a boat for many purposes, eg seizing shrouds to crosstrees, shackle pins, serving splices, etc. **4.** It is important to choose a type of copper ferrule that is compatible with the die of your swaging tool. **5.** This light, compact type of swage is recommended, even though it does take more time to complete the operation. **7.** This type of pop riveter is particularly well suited for work aloft, since it can be used with one hand. Two spare heads for different rivet sizes are housed in the sides of the hand-grip.

THE TOOLS OF
CHAPTER 3

Legend:

1. Wire-cutters for wire up to 16 mm in diameter. **2.** Wire-cutters for wire up to 7 mm in diameter. **3.** Ormiston seizing wire. **4.** Stainless steel thimbles and Talurit copper ferrules. **5.** Swage for hand crimping Talurit ferrules up to 6 mm in diameter. **6.** Spanner for swage. **7.** Pop riveter. **8.** Monel rivets.

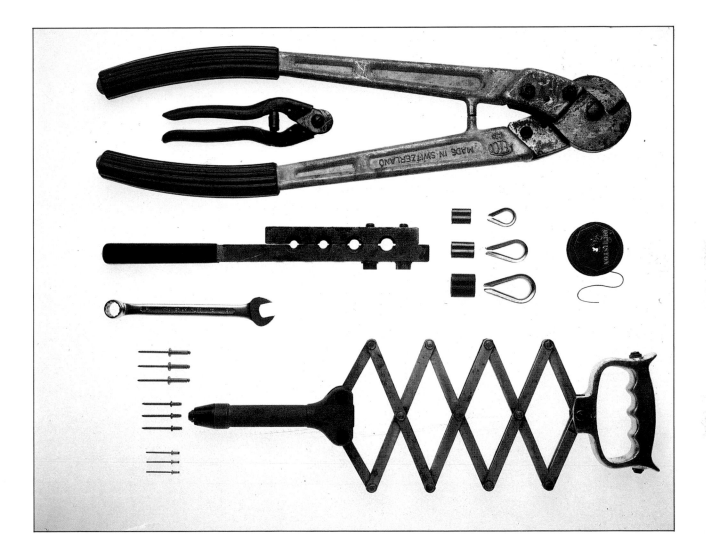

4. THE BOOM

Apart from being potentially lethal as it sweeps across the deck when gybing or tacking, to the jeopardy of the crew, the boom is the principal means of controlling the mainsail. With its various fittings, hardware and control systems, the boom is the mechanism for adjusting the mainsail shape rapidly and accurately in accordance with changes in wind direction and strength.

The boom is subject to severe stress and, as I have already implied, is suspended over the heads of the crew like a Sword of Damocles; it should be kept under constant surveillance, since proper and timely maintenance (both preventive and corrective) of all its associated equipment will reduce to a minimum the risk of regrettable accidents.

REEFING SYSTEMS

Booms can be divided into two main categories, depending on their reefing system: roller-reefing booms and fixed booms.

Booms of the first category usually have a circular cross-section and can be made to revolve around their axis by a set of gears operated by a crank handle; reefing is accomplished by wrapping the sail around the boom. This system, called the Appledore roller-reefing system, was first introduced during the nineteenth century to suit the fore-and-aft rig of British pilot cutters. The mainsail of these vessels, in fact, was cut straight to obtain a completely flat surface since the fullness of sail was controlled by the gaff. Present-day craft are all Bermudian-rigged, with the mainsail cut on the bias so as to incorporate a certain amount of fullness; as a result, numerous pleats and wrinkles form when you attempt to reef the sail around the boom and, when shaken out, the sail resembles a crumpled handkerchief. In addition, the system creates problems for the kicking strap and for the mainsheet; it is prone to jamming and is excessively slow. Altogether, roller-reefing

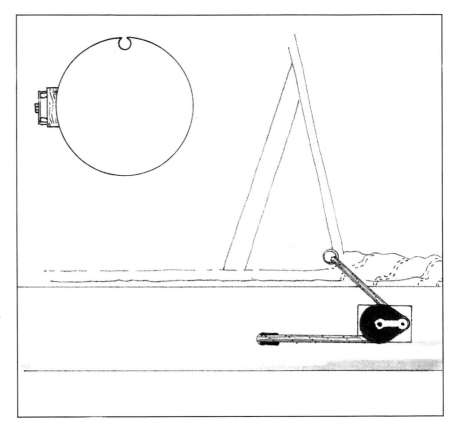

The drawing shows a method of obtaining the correct lead for the third or fourth reef pennant so that the reefed mainsail is trimmed correctly, with the clew cringle close to the boom and the foot and leech good and taut. The detail (top left) shows the shaped wooden block required for fixing the block to the curved surface of the boom.

is out-moded – unless, of course, your boat is gaff-rigged.

Fixed booms are of hollow construction and usually have an oval or rectangular cross-section as the greatest stresses occur in the upper and lower portions of the cross-sectional area. The reef pennants can be made to run either inside the boom or along its side. The best solution is probably a combination of the two: (i) three lines (clew outhaul, first and second reef pennant) running inside the boom and controlled by stoppers mounted on the underside of the boom near the gooseneck; (ii) the third and fourth reef pennants either running along the sides or entering the boom at a certain point from where they are led to the stoppers near the gooseneck.

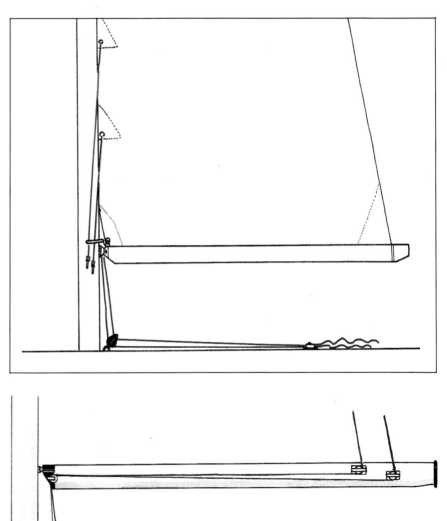

Above: schematic drawing of system for taking in reefs from the cockpit. Each luff pennant is fastened to an eye on the side of the mast, reeved through the cringle and taken to the cockpit via a fiddle block at the mast foot. The two falls of each pennant must be reeved through a ring, as shown in the figure, so that the cringle will remain close to the mast track when the pennant is hauled tight.
Below: modification of revolving boom. The drawing shows a solution with two reef pennants running externally along the boom via leading blocks fixed to it.

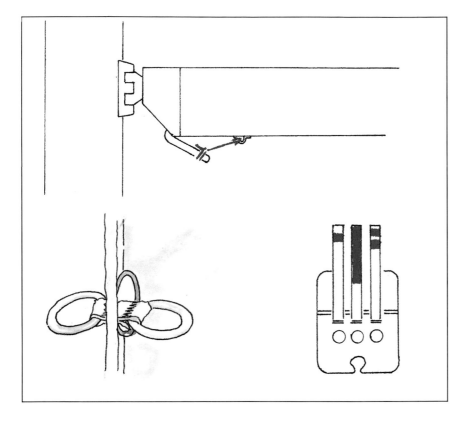

Roller-reefing booms can be modified by locking the gear mechanism and installing a set of leading blocks on the side of the boom for the reef-pennants. Mainsails, in this case, will need the addition of reinforced cringles at each row of reef points and are often bought already fitted with these extra items. Incidentally, don't forget the battens!

Here are some simple practical tips to make life easier when reefing. Mark the pennants or stoppers with bands of different coloured adhesive tape or with indelible felt-tip pens so that they can be identified immediately. Attach a pair of lazy rings to the luff reef cringles so as to make it easier to attach them to the reef hook. Splice on a lighter line to the higher reef pennants so as to facilitate operation and save on weight (see Chapter 5). Fit shock-cord retaining strops which can be hitched over the stopper levers so that there is no risk of a stopper jamming while shaking out a reef.

If the idea of taking in reefs without having to leave the cockpit appeals to you, you can adopt the following system – always provided that it is compatible with your deck layout. In the first place, the reef pennants must be led to

Above: stopper lever retainer. To prevent accidental closing of stoppers when shaking out reefs, it is advisable to fit short retaining strops of shock cord on the underside of the boom which can be hitched onto the stopper levers, as shown in the drawing.
Below left: luff cringle rings. These steel rings are attached to the luff reef cringle using a band of tubular webbing sewn as in the figure; the rings facilitate hitching the cringle to the hook at the gooseneck and also improve the set of the mainsail luff.
Below right: reef pennant marking. A good method for facilitating identification of reef pennants is to mark the stopper handles, using different-coloured strips of adhesive tape or indelible felt-tip pens.

the cockpit winches via fiddle blocks at the foot of the mast and stoppers placed within easy reach. For the luff, it is sufficient to reeve lines through the cringles which are then made fast to the mast at one end and led from the mast foot to the cockpit via leading blocks. Hauling in these lines requires no great effort and there is no need for a winch, while jamming cleats can be used instead of stoppers. This system, however, should only be used for the first two reefs; otherwise you risk making your cockpit an absolute jungle of ropes.

BOOM HARDWARE

The means of attachment of boom to mast must be particularly robust since it has to withstand high stresses. Many boats are fitted with a hinged gooseneck mounted on a track for vertical adjustment; this arrangement is acceptable for small craft, but is decidedly inadvisable for larger boats.

The gooseneck should incorporate a ball joint so that the boom is free to swing, lift or drop as required without impediment. In

addition, the assembly should be reinforced on either side (especially if the boat is fitted with a hydraulic kicking strap) and should preferably be fastened to the mast with screws. Apart from being stronger than rivets, screws permit easy dismantling for maintenance and repair.

The mainsheet purchase must be positioned correctly and work efficiently at all angles of sail trim and mast rake. If you decide that the number of parts is inadequate for developing the required power, an easy remedy is to reeve the

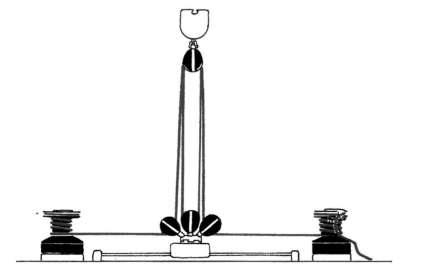

A mainsheet system for two winches, mainly suitable for racing boats.

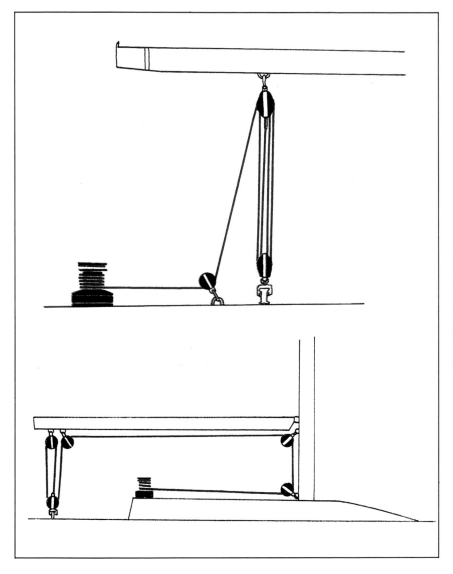

sheet through an additional block fixed to the underside of the boom; this arrangement will also spread the load more evenly along the boom. Blocks attached to the boom should be of the fixed type, since swivel blocks tend to twist the sheet around itself; if you have nothing but swivel blocks on board, the swivel can be locked with a length of lanyard.

The main clew outhaul is also subject to severe stress and frequently gives rise to problems. It is advisable to lash the main clew cringle to a slider or, on larger boats, to a car on a track which permits trimming the foot of the sail under any wind conditions. What is important is to see that the main clew stays well aligned with the foot of the sail and that sufficient travel is provided to carry out necessary adjustments.

Other types of mainsheet system to suit different deck layouts.

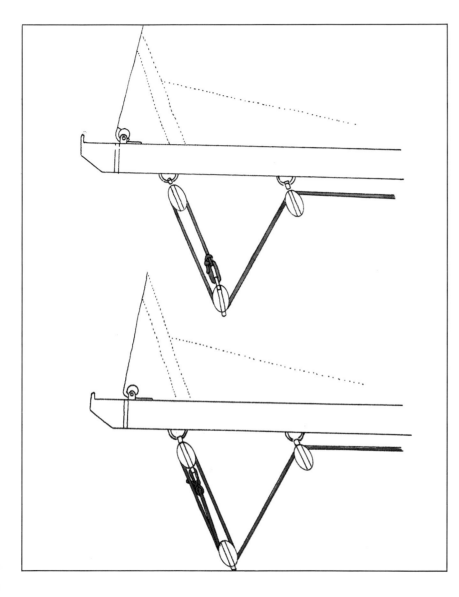

Left: modified mainsheet purchase. The purchase shown in the upper sketch is modified by removing the single block on the boom and fitting the foot block in its place, with the addition of a double block (see lower sketch).

Below: swivel blocks can be locked with one or two turns of tubular tape or line, as shown in the figure.

THE KICKING STRAP

This useful means of controlling the height of the boom and the set of the mainsail is only too often (and mistakenly) considered as optional for cruising boats. Various types of kicking strap are available, suitable for every type of boat and for their specific requirements. Correct handling of the kicking strap will improve to a noticeable degree the performance of a boat on any point of sailing.

A purchase fitted with jamming cleats is undoubtedly the most frequently encountered type of kicking strap; it should be installed with the cleats on the side of the boom to facilitate adjustment and to ensure a quick release when letting go. Lever types can also be found, consisting of a purchase and an adjustable arm, as well as solid kicking straps with an adjuster wheel which operate on the same principle as the backstay adjuster.

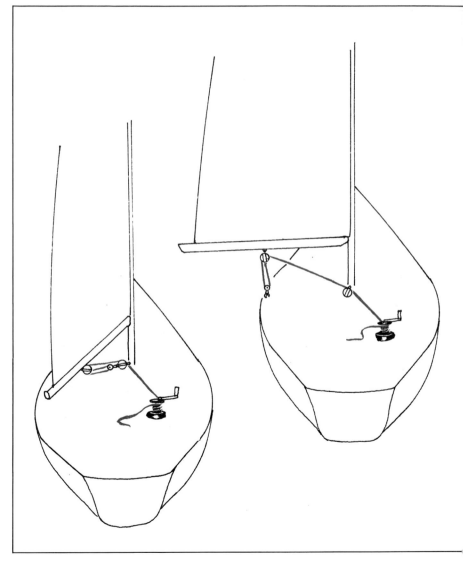

Right: the two drawings show a kicking strap system which can be easily rerigged as a preventer when running before the wind.
On opposite page: example of how the spinnaker downhaul can be used as a preventer.

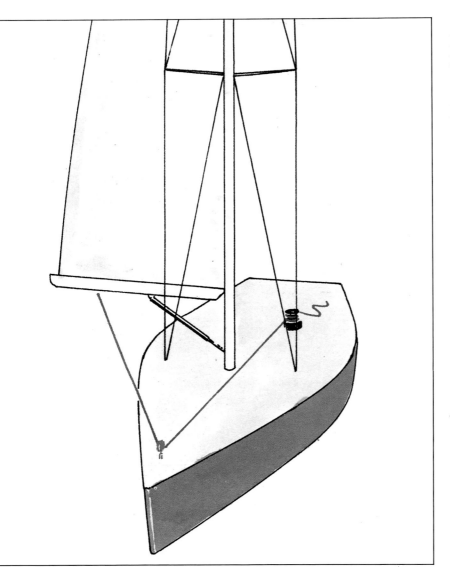

Finally, there are the hydraulic kicking straps. Although principally used on racing boats, these kicking straps in point of fact are also of great interest to the keen cruising enthusiast as they permit fine, stepless trimming of the mainsail, require no particular attention and provide sufficient support for the boom for it to be possible to dispense with the tiresome topping lift.

The lever and solid types of kicking strap can develop powerful loads and must therefore be provided with strong, well-designed anchorages. The bracket on the mast must be strong enough to withstand torsional stresses and include a knuckle joint, while its shaped base-plate should wrap some way around the mast and be fixed to it with screws. The same criteria apply to the connection to the boom, except that the knuckle joint can be omitted as long as the hinge is correctly positioned for the boom to rise and fall freely.

SPINNAKER POLE

One – or even two – spinnaker poles, well secured, are prominently displayed on the deck of many a cruising yacht at her berth, but are rarely called upon when the boat is at sea. This is due in part to a widespread prejudice against the spinnaker and in part to the insufficient experience of the average cruising yachtsman in working this particular headsail. It is true that correct handling of the spinnaker calls for a certain flair and much application, but it is equally true that use of the spinnaker can give a great deal of pleasure and excitement as well as a vastly superior performance when a boat is off the wind.

A well-designed spinnaker pole is possibly the best incentive for encouraging a more frequent use of this truly spectacular sail. First of all, the spinnaker pole must be of the right length (approximately equal to the distance between the foot of the mast and the base of the forestay). If the pole is too long, cut a piece off the end and drill and thread new holes for the fastening screws of end fitting; if the pole is instead too short, you can use the sleeving technique, also used in the case of cracks or fractures.

Spinnaker pole and fittings. *Left*: this type of inboard end fitting incorporates a spring latch system for attachment to the mast and is suitable for medium-size to large boats. *Right*: view of outboard end fitting showing the two rings for fastening spinnaker pole topping lift and downhaul, the open spring catch and (in the middle) the mechanism that snaps the jaws shut.

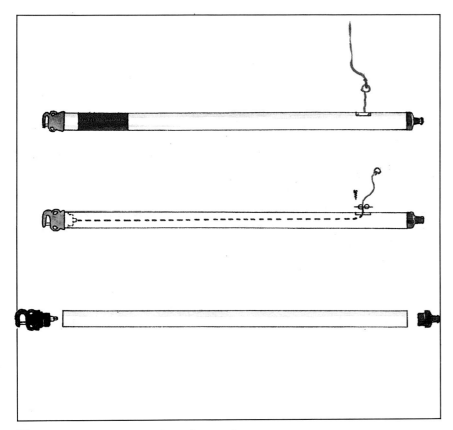

How to construct a spinnaker pole

Once you have acquired the right type of inboard and outboard end fitting for your boat and selected a piece of light alloy tube (cut to the required length and with the right diameter for the end fittings), cut a slot in the tube a short distance from the inner end and poke free end of the spring plunger release line through the slot, pulling it out through the outer end of the pole. Connect line to plunger, apply sealing compound to both end fittings, fit them in position and fix with machine screws. Complete the job by covering the boom with a protective leather sheath where it is usually in contact with the shrouds. If the ring on the control line is out of reach, attach a lanyard to it.

On smaller boats, the spinnaker boom is generally secured to a ring mounted on the mast at a fixed height and the two ends of the pole, both outboard and inboard, are identical. Make sure that (a) the ring is sufficiently strong and firmly fixed (if necessary, replace rivets with screws), and (b) the inner end fitting is of a size compatible with that of the ring so as to prevent any possible mutual damage, with consequent failure of the one or the other component. For larger boats, it is preferable to have a slider travelling on a track fixed to the mast and fitted with a spigot or with a bell fitting (depending on the type of end fitting on the pole) which permits adjustment of the height of the boom above the deck; in this case, the outer end of the pole is fitted with a spring-loaded plunger that acts as a catch. All these mechanical components must be kept clean and free from salt deposits, and lubricated every so often with a drop or two of oil. It is also very important to make sure that the end fitting has a smooth finish, without sharp edges or roughness which could lead to premature wear of the spinnaker guy.

Finishing touches to the spinnaker pole should include a leather protective sheath around the section which comes more frequently into contact with the forestay when reaching and a lanyard attached to the ring controlling the plunger on the outer end.

JOCKEY POLE

This term is used to indicate the short tubular bearing-out spar which serves to widen the angle between the spinnaker guy and pole on a reach.

It is an extremely useful device in that it reduces considerably the compression force acting on the pole and limits pole wear. If your boat is not equipped with a jockey pole, you can make one yourself quite easily.

Take a piece of light-alloy tubing (a discarded mast or boom of an old dinghy will do very well), cut off a length approximately equal to half the maximum beam of your boat and seal the open ends with a pair of plastic end fittings made to take the guy and the mast eye. A stout eye plate fixed to the mast with screws is sufficient for the inner connection, one on each side.

As a finishing touch, put a protective leather sheath around the jockey pole at the point where it rests against the shrouds; in any case, it is always wiser to pad the pole where it is lashed to the shrouds.

CONCLUSION

Booms, spinnaker poles and jockey poles should be rinsed thoroughly and frequently with fresh water to remove all traces of salt, while their movable components must be lubricated periodically with the same mixture described for winches or, alternatively, with a Teflon spray.

When the boat is laid up, it is good practice to remove the reef pennants from the boom and replace them with suitable messengers; in addition, it is advisable to remove the mainsheet and the kicking strap, replacing them with any unwanted lengths of rope.

How to mend a broken spinnaker pole

The drawings show (from top to bottom) the sequence of operations to be carried out. *1*. Measure original length of broken pole. *2*. Cut off jagged ends with hacksaw; to make sure you cut at right angle, wrap a sheet of newspaper around the boom, check that the edges are perfectly aligned and draw a line around the pole. *3*. Choose two lengths of tube: the first must have exactly the same diameter (inside and outside) as the pole, while the second must have an external diameter slightly smaller than the internal diameter of the pole so as to obtain a snug fit. Cut the first piece to the exact length of the missing section of the pole. *4*. Push the smaller tube through the larger one and fix in place with rivets or screws, leaving on each side a length equal to at least 2–3 times the external diameter of the pole. *5*. Final assembly consists in pushing the protruding ends of the smaller tube into the two sections of the original pole and fixing them in place with a series of rivets, as in the drawing. Self-tapping screws are preferable in the case of boats over 30 ft (9 m). Do not forget, before assembly, to pass the release line back through the pole.

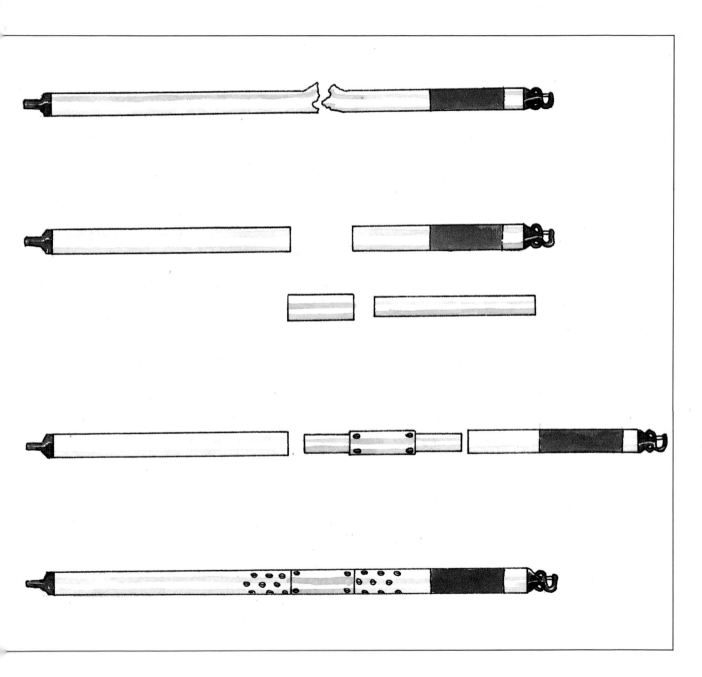

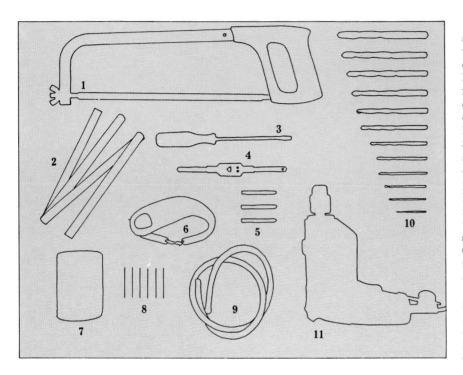

1. Choose a heavy-duty type. The one shown in the photograph is adjustable and takes blades of different lengths. Use top-quality blades and replace fequently. Blades must be fitted with teeth facing forward, since the hacksaw should cut during the forward movement. 2. This type of folding rule is of stainless steel and is highly practical in that it will not rust. 3. Always choose a good make; Bahco screwdrivers from Sweden are excellent. 4. In addition to the type shown in the photograph, there is a chuck type with T handle which is extremely practical for use in a boat. 5. Buy one set at a time as and when you need them; you need only a second tap to thread aluminium. 6/7/8. See Chapter 1, page 22 (notes 4, 7, 5). 9. Keep on board a few metres of the more commonly used diameters (4, 6, 8 mm). 10. Use high-speed bits and sharpen them frequently. 11. In addition to the standard mains electric drill, it is very useful to have a battery-powered model on board; Makita makes first-class battery-powered portable drills.

THE TOOLS OF CHAPTER 4

Legend:

1. Hacksaw. 2. Folding steel rule. 3. Screwdriver. 4. Tap wrench. 5. Set of taps. 6. Sailmaker's palm. 7. Waxed thread. 8. Sailmaker's needles. 9. Shock cord. 10. High-speed drill bits. 11. Portable electric drill.

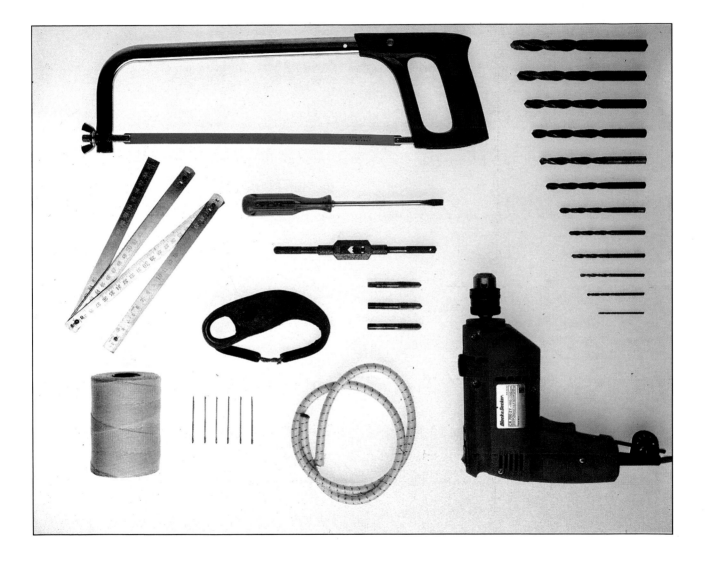

5. RUNNING RIGGING

The running rigging of a yacht includes halyards, sheets, topping lifts, downhauls, reef pennants, kicking strap and any other rope used for setting and trimming the sails.

Just as the name of a rope varies according to its function, its construction also often varies according to the use for which it is intended. It is essential that the right type of rope is used for each particular task: only in this way can high performance and long service, with acceptable safety margins, be obtained from running rigging.

It is often said that you can judge a seaman by the state of his ropes, which reflects the vital importance of good running rigging for a sailing vessel. Never try to economise on ropes: there is practically no limit to their useful life on a boat. They are real perennials and can be used over and over again for progressively less strenuous jobs.

HALYARDS

The choice available in this field has been considerably broadened by the introduction of Kevlar and other man-made fibres. As a rule the mainsail halyard is of the rope-and-wire type, since there is little to recommend all-wire halyards and their awkward and occasionally dangerous winches.

The rope tail generally has a diameter around three times that of the stainless steel (7 × 19 strand) or galvanised wire halyard to which it is attached. Galvanised wire is more flexible, has a longer life and is less apt to become brittle; at times, however, it can be subject to rusting.

An alternative solution is to use all-rope halyards (of the Kevlar or pre-stretched type) which do not give rise to winch problems like wire and which are also both easier to handle and less dangerous for the hands. In addition, they are

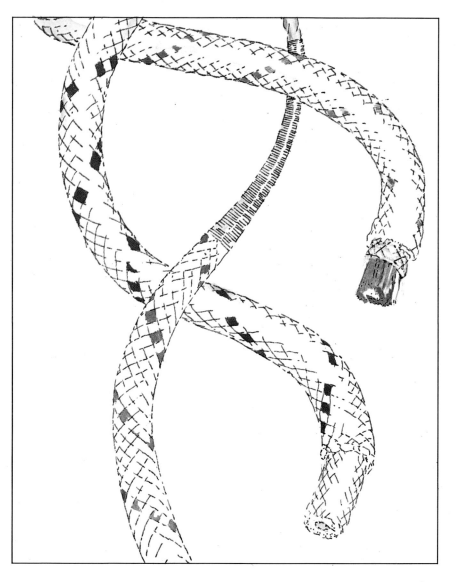

The splice joining a wire halyard to a rope tail is shown in the centre of the figure. The green-speckled rope, used for the splice, is of the plaited double-braid type; the red-speckled rope is a Kevlar rope with parallel-filament core and can be used without wire for an all-rope halyard.

slightly less heavy and permit the use of light-alloy winch drums, with a resulting reduction of the all-up weight of the boat.

A part wire, part rope halyard is the best choice for the genoa or, alternatively, you can use a Kevlar rope. Kevlar is an aramid fibre, a fairly new material for ropes, that is 20 times stronger than steel wire of equal diameter; however, when twisted into strands and laid into a rope, it tends to wear rather rapidly and, in addition, can lose up to 70 per cent of its original

strength around sharp bends. For these reasons, Kevlar ropes generally have a parallel-filament aramid fibre core protected by one or two plaited polyester sheaths. The sheaths not only increase the bending radius of the rope over sheaves and leading blocks, but also protect the core against abrasion and ultraviolet rays (to which Kevlar is highly sensitive).

Kevlar ropes are still a fairly costly item compared to conventional man-made fibre ropes and this has limited their use up to now

to highly sophisticated racing craft. It is good practice, however, to carry a spare halyard of this type on board which, in case of necessity, can be used either for the mainsail or for the genoa. (The comments relating to the genoa halyard apply equally to staysail halyards.)

You can use a pre-stretched rope of suitable size for the spinnaker halyard, or else a slightly larger size of double-braid sheet line which is less stiff and does not have the tiresome tendency (typical of

BREAKING LOAD (kg)								
Diameter (mm)	Galvanized steel flexible wire 7 × 19		Kevlar rope		Parallel-filament core plaited polyester rope		Double-braid rope	
	(lb)	(kg)	(lb)	(kg)	(lb)	(kg)	(lb)	(kg)
4	2290	1040	–	–	1045	475	–	–
5	3590	1630	1320	600	–	–	–	–
6	5180	2350	2090	950	1270	575	1430	650
7	7050	3200	–	–	–	–	–	–
8	9260	4200	3860	1750	2340	1060	2590	1175
9	11700	5310	–	–	–	–	–	–
10	14000	6570	5700	2600	4590	2080	3970	1800
12	20800	9450	7700	3500	6110	2770	5680	2575
14	28400	12900	12600	5700	8820	4000	8050	3650
16	37000	16800	–	–	13000	5900	9980	4525
18	47000	21300	–	–	15500	7030	12500	5675
20	57800	26200	–	–	18300	8300	17500	7925

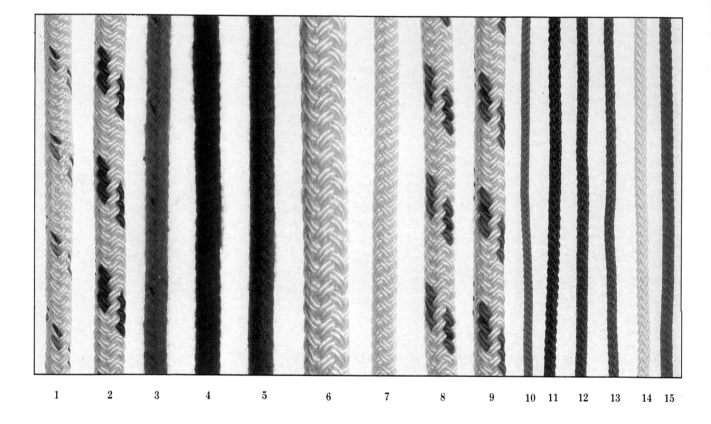

Various types of rope. *1–2* Pre-stretched plaited double-braid polyester ropes, used for mixed wire-and-rope halyards, for reef-pennants and downhauls. *3–5* Plaited double-braid short-fibre polyester ropes, used for sheets in general (small boats) and for light spinnaker sheets (larger boats). *6–7* Plaited double-braid polyester ropes, used for genoa and spinnaker sheets, topping lifts and spinnaker halyards. *8–9* Parallel-filament core plaited polyester ropes (low stretch), used for spinnaker guys, all-rope halyards and in some cases for downhauls and reef pennants. *10–15* Small-diameter plaited polyester ropes for sundry uses.

pre-stretched ropes) of kinking, a serious handicap when the halyard has to be paid out fast to lower the spinnaker in double-quick time.

The wire section of wire-and-rope halyards should be long enough to permit leaving at least three or four turns on the winch after the sail has been hoisted to the masthead. Foresails which are not hoisted to the full height of the forestay should be equipped with wire spans of suitable length, so that the shackle of the halyard is always hoisted right up to the masthead. In the case of the main-sail, remember to increase the length of the wire section sufficiently to allow for reefing. The rope section of the halyard should be long enough to permit taking two or three turns on the winch when the shackle of the halyard is still lying on the deck; increase the length by a yard or two, both for making fast and as a reserve for when the rope starts showing patches of wear and has to be shortened.

If used correctly, good-quality halyards can last almost indefinitely; they should therefore be checked at regular intervals for signs of incipient wear which may point to the misalignment of a

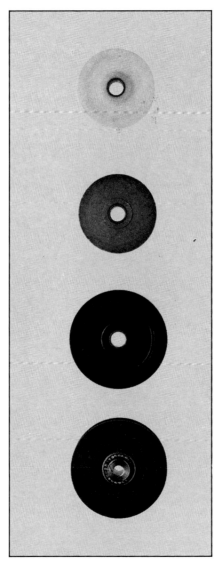

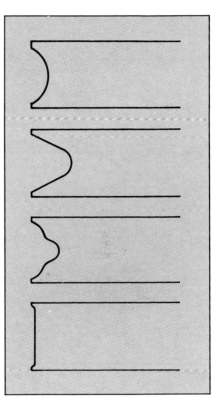

Types of sheave. *Left, from top to bottom*: synthetic sheave, two light-alloy sheaves, ball-bearing mounted sheave. *Right, from top to bottom*: groove profiles for different types of rope: rope, wire, wire and rope, Kevlar rope.

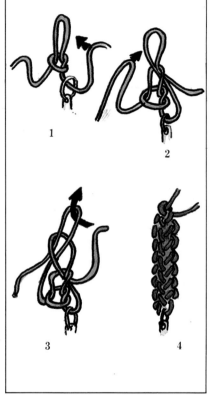

sheave or leading block, to a damaged sheave or even to chafing against another halyard owing to accidental crossing of the two ropes within the mast.

When you want to check the entire length of the halyard that runs inside the mast, fasten the end of the halyard to the shackle and hoist the halyard as if it were attached to the mainsail. Since the ends of the halyard are tied together, you can haul out the entire section up to the splice (if the halyard is of the rope-and-wire type) onto the deck for inspection and then run it back again up the mast by hauling the shackle down. The remaining part of the halyard can be lowered onto the deck for inspection by fastening a messenger to the end of the halyard and hauling on the shackle end. Remember to attach the messenger very firmly if you wish to avoid an unscheduled trip to the masthead!

This knot for attaching a lanyard to the ring of a snap shackle is a practical way of forming a short strop for opening the shackle; it is a very easy knot and permits opening of the shackle under any conditions.

Left: genoa halyard fitted with a small bead that prevents the splice from jamming in the masthead sheave.

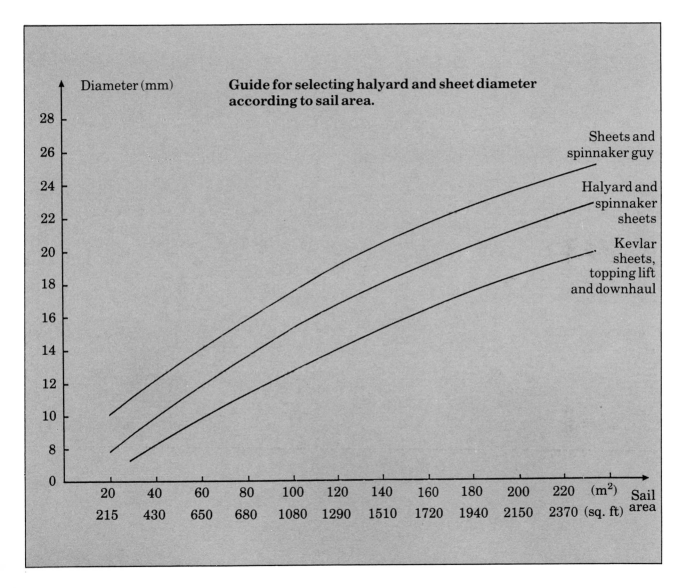

Diameter (mm)

Guide for selecting halyard and sheet diameter according to sail area.

Sheets and spinnaker guy

Halyard and spinnaker sheets

Kevlar sheets, topping lift and downhaul

Sail area

SHEETS

These ropes must be flexible, strong, easy to coil and, above all, must be used exclusively as sheets! Never give way to the temptation of seizing the nearby genoa sheet when, in port, you want to take a spring either to a nearby boat or to a bollard on the quay.

Double-braided rope is the most suitable type for all sheets. The size of the rope will vary depending on the size of the sail. For mainsail and foresail sheets, always choose the maximum diameter indicated for the area of the sail; in the case of the spinnaker, however, it can be an advantage to have two sets of sheets (one light and one heavy) and switch from the one to the other according to wind speed and direction. It is preferable to use a pre-stretched, parallel-filament core rope for the spinnaker guy (one of the best is Gleistein's Cup Sheet) as this type of rope has a very low coefficient of elasticity and will hold the spinnaker pole firmly in place.

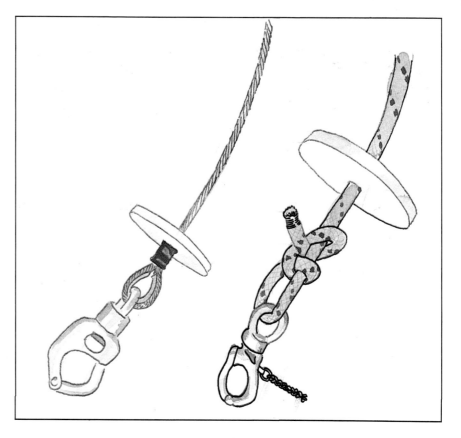

Two alternatives for the spinnaker guy. *Left*: wire (with a rope tail) fitted with a high-strength Sparcraft snap shackle. *Right*: pre-stretched rope secured to a conventional snap shackle by means of two half-hitches. In both cases the snap shackle is held at the right angle by a plastic disc, which also prevents the shackle from fouling the spinnaker pole end fitting.

How to serve a rope

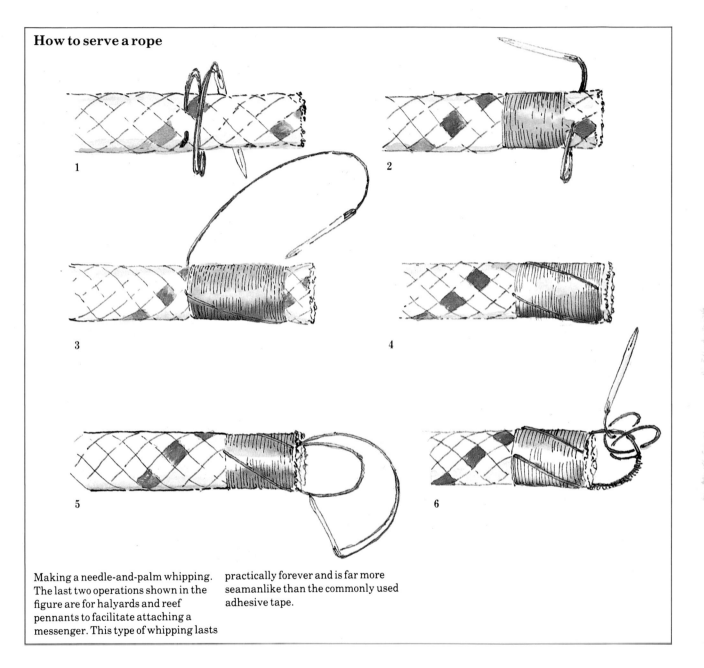

1

2

3

4

5

6

Making a needle-and-palm whipping. The last two operations shown in the figure are for halyards and reef pennants to facilitate attaching a messenger. This type of whipping lasts practically forever and is far more seamanlike than the commonly used adhesive tape.

TOPPING LIFTS

Almost all masts are fitted on the aft side with a second masthead sheave which is for the topping lift for the main boom. This is possibly the most convenient solution, as the topping lift can also be used as a messenger should it be necessary at sea to rig a jury halyard for the mainsail. An alternative solution is to fix the lift to the masthead and terminate it a short distance above the boom; connection to the boom is made by a purchase with the fall running inside the boom and exiting from the side to be made fast to a cleat. Both solutions are valid, although in the second case the topping lift is less easy to handle when the mainsail is reefed.

For the main boom, the topping lift can be either a small-diameter

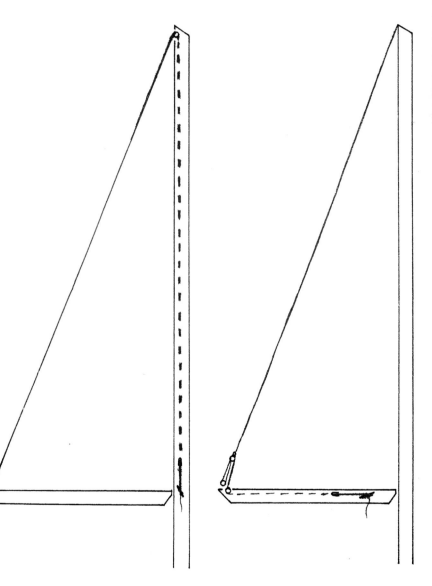

Two alternative arrangements for the topping lift. *Left*: generally using a small-diameter rope, the lift is fixed to the boom, looped over the sheave at the masthead and led down inside the mast to a slot from which it exits and is made fast to a cleat. *Right*: a small-diameter wire topping lift is fixed to the masthead and terminated some distance above the boom where it is attached to a purchase, the hauling part of which is led along inside the boom.

wire with a rope tail or a continuous rope of suitable size; a standard double-braided rope is sufficient for the spinnaker pole topping lift, since once the sail is drawing it keeps the pole up by itself.

DOWNHAULS

Unlike the topping lift, the spinnaker pole downhaul is under constant stress since its task is to restrain the spinnaker pole against the force of the sail. What is needed, therefore, is a pre-stretched rope with very low elasticity and a stout leading block fixed at the bows; in addition, the downhaul must be taken to a winch so that it can be hauled really taut if the wind freshens or in a choppy sea.

When the boat is used purely for cruising, the spinnaker pole topping lift and downhaul can both be attached to the rings on the boom arm by means of knots and there is no need for snap shackles.

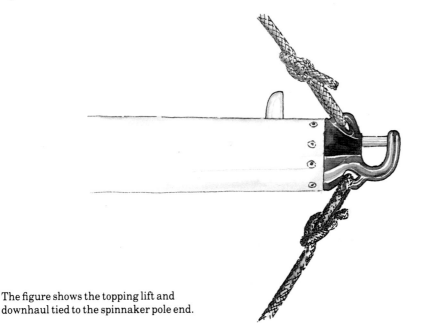

The figure shows the topping lift and downhaul tied to the spinnaker pole end.

REEF PENNANTS

These ropes are particularly important since they are used for adjusting the trim of the mainsail in anything from a strong breeze to a near gale. The type of rope recommended for reef pennants is a pre-stretched double-braid rope with parallel-filament core (like Gleistein's Cup Sheet); a very low stretch is an essential quality for pennants so that they flatten the mainsail correctly in a strong wind.

Although the strain exerted on the reef pennant decreases as the sail is progressively shortened by taking in reefs, it is good practice (especially when the wind shows signs of freshening) to secure the mainsail with a strop passed once or twice through the reef cringle and around the boom. This simple precaution may save you a lot of trouble later on.

A practical method for avoiding unnecessary weighing-down of the mainsail, and for reducing the length of the reef pennants is to reeve the upper reef pennants (third and fourth) only when they are actually needed – that is, after the first two reefs have been taken in. A small diameter messenger is used for this purpose, looped per-

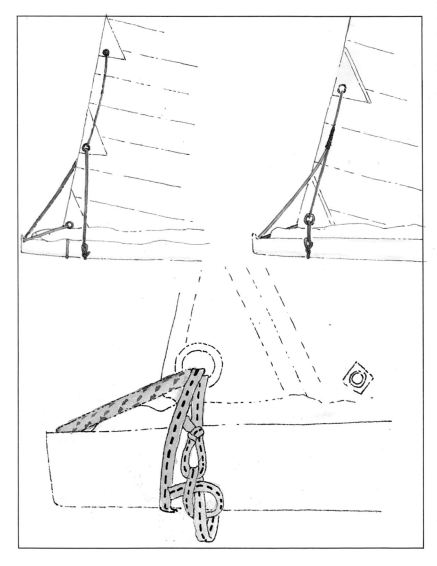

manently between the adjacent upper reef cringles. In addition, the second reef pennant (which is generally kept permanently reeved) can be shortened and spliced, at the inboard end, to a suitable length of flexible rope of smaller size; the length of this rope tail must be sufficient to ensure that the pennant proper will reach the winch before the winch starts hauling the sail taut. Since the flexible rope is easier to handle than the pre-stretched rope used for the pennant, the sail can be reefed with greater rapidity and, at the same time, it is possible to continue to use reef pennants which have had to be shortened owing to wear.

Another useful measure is to mark the earring ends with different-coloured strips of adhesive tape or indelible felt-tip pens so that they can be identified immediately (see Chapter 4).

Reef pennants. *Above*: the drawings show a small messenger rove between the upper reef cringles; when the reef pennant has to be reeved, it is taped temporarily to the messenger and pulled through the cringle. *Below*: reef cringle lashed for safety. Use strong tape or lanyard since the lashing is subject to heavy loads.

On many yachts, the winch for the reef pennants is fixed onto the aft side of the mast or to the underside of the boom. These systems usually turn out to be impractical and it is best either to remove the winch and re-install it in a more suitable position on deck or to use another, existing winch at the foot of the mast; in the latter case, the pennants are led to the winch by way of a fiddle block near the foot of the mast and via, if necessary, suitable stoppers.

Method of attaching reef pennants. *Above*: correct (left) and incorrect (right) way of tying reef pennant around the boom. *Below*: depending on how the mainsail is bent to the boom, pennant will be rigged as shown in the right- or left-hand sketch.

KICKING STRAP AND RUNNERS

Any type of strong, high-grade rope can be used for the kicking strap, preventer and tackles in general, provided that the rope is not too stiff and runs smoothly around the sheaves. Sound lengths of worn-out sheets or halyard rope tails which have become too short can be utilised successfully.

An exception must be made for the runners on fractional-rigged boats. In this case, a high-strength rope must be used, the only alternative being wire (which is, however, more awkward to handle). All things considered, a high-quality pre-stretched rope or, for larger boats, a rope with parallel-filament core that has a very low stretch are the best choice. It should not be necessary to add that this is certainly not the moment to economise over the price: after all, what is at stake is the well-being of your mast!

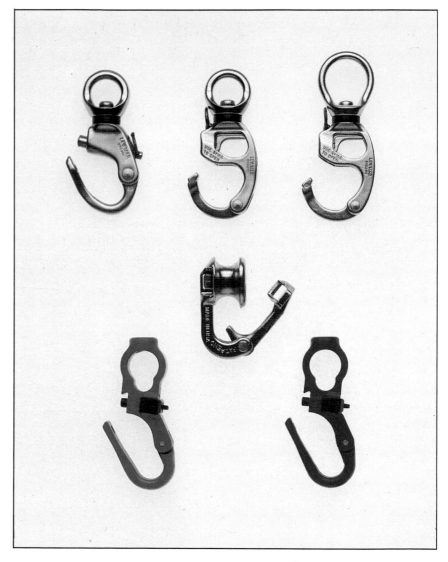

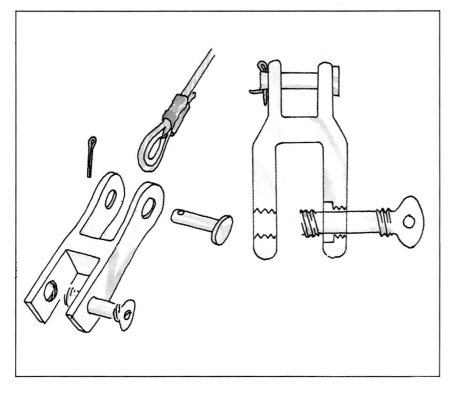

Top, from left to right: swivel snap shackles for halyards, spinnaker sheet and spinnaker guy. *Centre*: this type is especially suitable for genoa sheets, much used on racing boats. *Below*: plastic snap shackles for lightweight spinnaker sheets. *On this page*: this type of shackle, if it can be obtained, is ideal for the mainsail halyard. It has several good points: it can be connected directly to an eye splice; it can be opened and closed easily and rapidly by means of the threaded pin; the threading of both lugs prevents the pin from falling out.

GENERAL REFLECTIONS ON ROPES

There is such a wide range of cordage for nautical use on the market today that the owners of pleasure boats may well find themselves in difficulties when deciding what to buy.

It is worthwhile emphasising once again the highly important role played by running rigging in relation to the performance of your craft, as well as to the safety of craft and crew.

Economic considerations cannot of course be wholly ignored, but neither should they eclipse all other criteria when it comes to making your choice. Buy less rope if you cannot afford to spend much, but always choose top-quality rope. High-grade sheets and halyards will last far longer, give better service and will prove, in the long run, to be a better investment.

Leading rope manufacturers on the world market are the German firm Gleistein and the two American firms Samson and Yale. The French firm Lancelin also produces high-quality ropes and, in Britain, Marlow and Bridon.

All the ropes mentioned so far in

How to coil a rope

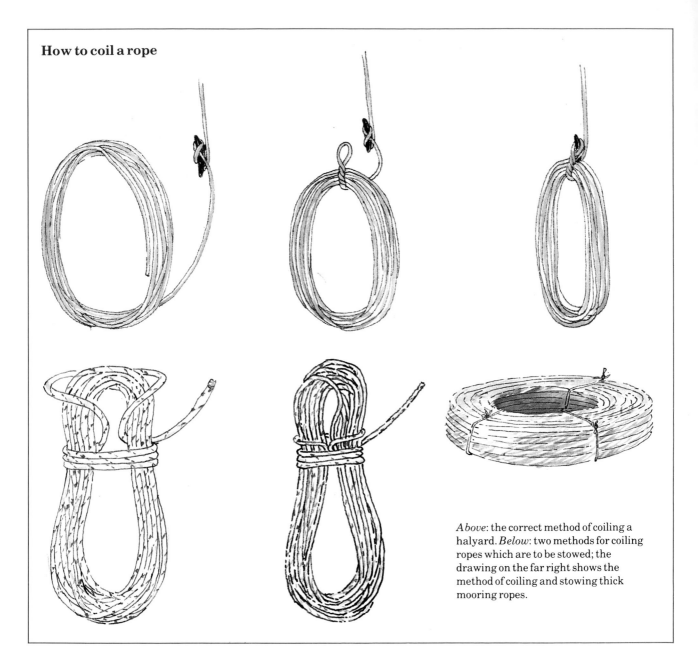

Above: the correct method of coiling a halyard. *Below*: two methods for coiling ropes which are to be stowed; the drawing on the far right shows the method of coiling and stowing thick mooring ropes.

this chapter (with the exception of Kevlar ropes) are made of polyester fibre and are supplied commercially under various trade names (Dacron, Tergal, Terylene, etc). Roughly speaking, they can be divided into two main categories according to their surface texture. Ropes in the first category have a smooth, slightly shiny surface, due to the impregnated polyester filaments of which they are made; they also absorb less water and are resistant to wear (a quality that makes these ropes particularly suited for use with winches). Ropes of the second category are rounder in shape and more compact; they also have a fuzzy surface, deriving from the short-fibre polyester filaments of which the strands are made, that renders them more prone to wear. For this reason, these ropes are less recommended, particularly for use with self-tailing winches.

WARPS AND MOORING LINES

Mooring lines are another fundamental item of ship's gear, since the safety of your boat is often directly dependent on the quality of these ropes.

As a rule, polyester or polyamide laid (three-strand) or plaited (eight-strand) ropes are used for mooring lines. These ropes are strong, easily spliced and usually less expensive than double-braid ropes. The eight-strand plaited type has two main advantages: it does not form kinks and is fairly resistant to wear. In addition, it does not slip easily and for this reason is very suitable for the anchor cable. Polyamide fibre ropes, better known as nylon ropes, are slightly less strong than polyester ropes and have a tendency to shrink and harden when wet.

The normal complement of mooring lines for a boat should include two 30–50 ft (10–15 m) long painters, for making fast to the quay and from two to four slightly longer mooring lines 50–60 ft (15–20 m) for use as warps or springs. In addition, it is advisable to have on board a couple of very long lines 50–100 fathoms (50–100 m) which will almost certainly come in handy in harbour and at anchor, or even, sooner or later, for a tow. For the kedge anchor you can use an eight-strand plaited rope, at least 25 fathoms (50 m) long.

Other materials are used for mooring ropes besides polyester and polyamide fibres. One of these is Hardyhemp which, when twisted, closely resembles hemp; it

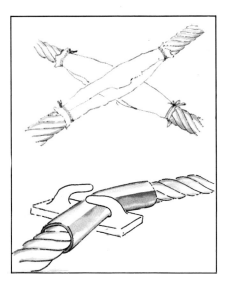

Two practical ways of protecting mooring lines against wear: the first uses cloth padding, the second a split length of soft plastic hose.

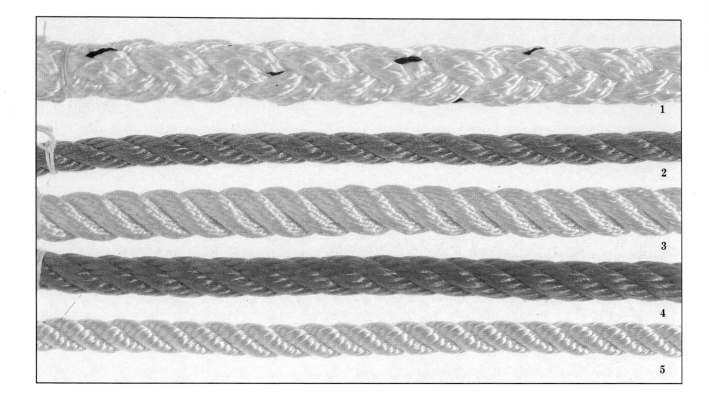

1. Plaited eight-strand polyamide rope, used for anchor cables and mooring lines. 2 & 4. Laid three-strand polypropylene ropes, elastic, buoyant and light, they are widely used as tow lines on ships, fishing boats and yachts. 3 & 5. Laid three-strand polyamide ropes, used exclusively as mooring lines – but expensive.

On opposite page: mooring knots. 1. Clove hitch and two half-hitches. 2. Continuous tackle for reaching the quay without having to adjust the mooring ropes. 3. Round turn and bowline. 4. Slippery hitch, this slightly cowboy-style knot can be used for temporarily tying up the tender and offers the advantage of being easily undone even at a distance.

is also highly resistant to chemicals, thanks to the high polypropylene content, and stays afloat if dropped into the water. Hempex ropes are very popular with everyone who likes the traditional look, but it should be borne in mind that their breaking load is 40 per cent less than that of polyester and polyamide fibre ropes.

Finally, there are three-strand laid polypropylene ropes which have a smooth and slightly fibrous appearance; they too are buoyant and consequently are particularly well suited for use as tow ropes. Remember that the length of the tow should be from four to six times the length of the boat, depending on weather and sea conditions. Polypropylene is sensitive to ultraviolet rays and its resistance consequently varies according to the colour of the rope; experimental tests have shown that black is the least affected colour, while orange tends to fade prematurely.

ANCHORS

Although there are scores of anchor designs on the market, it is always wiser to stick to the better-known types. The Admiralty pattern is probably the safest and most versatile type of anchor, even if it does present some handling and stowage problems. One of the most popular types is the CQR anchor which fits neatly over the stern and has good holding power, provided that the seabed is not too

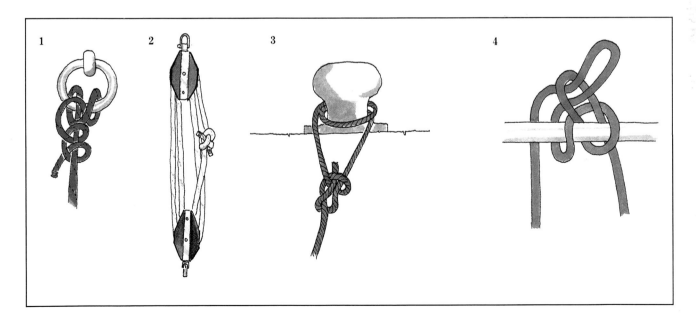

Method of sinking the anchor cable. In crowded anchorages it is often helpful to sink the anchor cable to a convenient depth, where it cannot be fouled by other boats. For this purpose, fix a suitable weight to a snatchblock and run the snatchblock down the cable under the control of a lanyard attached to the shackle.

hard. Care must be taken, however, when using this anchor to ensure that it digs firmly into the bottom. Never put your trust in one of the many imitations of this pattern: I did so once and narrowly escaped running ashore and losing my boat. The Danforth anchor is also very popular with cruising yachtsmen, despite its bulk, since it holds very well on sandy bottoms.

There are two principal factors which ensure that the anchor will take a firm hold on the seabed. In the first place, the anchor must be dropped correctly so that its flukes can dig deeply into the bottom; secondly, a sufficiently heavy anchor chain must be used so that the strain on the anchor remains horizontal, without the shank being lifted off the seabed when it comes under pressure.

If your boat is not equipped with an anchor winch and it is necessary to use a rope anchor cable, it is advisable to connect the rope to the anchor by means of at least 30–50 ft (10–15 m) of chain one size larger than that shown in the table.

LENGTH OF BOAT		ANCHOR WEIGHT						ANCHOR CHAIN			
		Admiralty		CQR		Danforth special steel		Minimum length		Link diameter	
(ft)	(m)	(lb)	(kg)	(lb)	(kg)	(lb)	(kg)	(ft)	(m)	(in)	(mm)
19.5–26.25	6–8	24	11	15	7	12	5.5	25	7	¼	7
26.25–39.5	8–12	40	18	25	12	20	9	40	12.5	⁵⁄₁₆	8
39.5–56	12–17	70	32	45	20	35	16	40	12.5	⅜	10
56–75.5	17–23	120	54	75	35	60	27	80	25	½	12
75.5–88.5	23–27	175	80	110	50	90	40	80	25	⁹⁄₁₆	14

Anchors

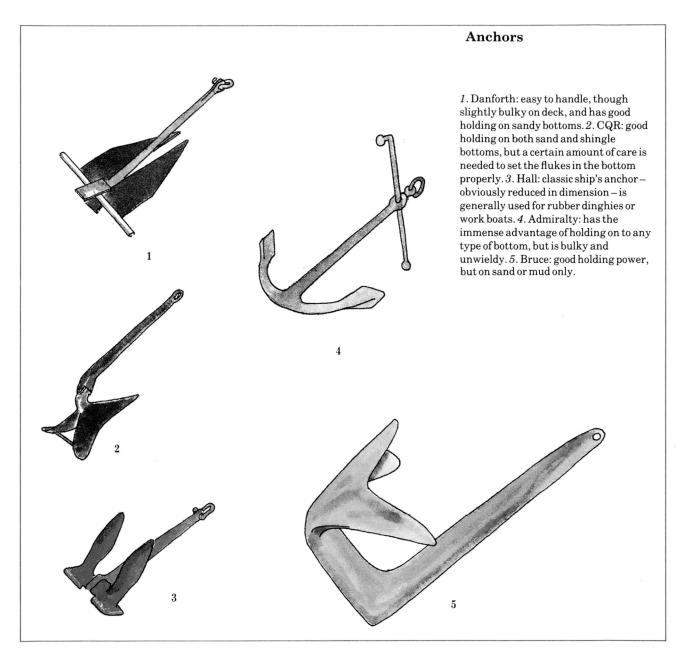

1. Danforth: easy to handle, though slightly bulky on deck, and has good holding on sandy bottoms. 2. CQR: good holding on both sand and shingle bottoms, but a certain amount of care is needed to set the flukes in the bottom properly. 3. Hall: classic ship's anchor – obviously reduced in dimension – is generally used for rubber dinghies or work boats. 4. Admiralty: has the immense advantage of holding on to any type of bottom, but is bulky and unwieldy. 5. Bruce: good holding power, but on sand or mud only.

1

2

3

4

5

A

B

Splices: eye splice on three-strand rope

A. Bind rope tightly with adhesive tape at a distance of 8–10 in (20–25 cm) from its end, unlay the rope up to the binding and bind the ends of the three strands with different coloured tapes. Insert fid into rope, from right to left as shown. Tuck strands one at a time: first the red, then the yellow and finally the green.

B. On completion of the first set of tucks, the three strands should all emerge from the rope at the same point, forming equal angles of approximately 120 degrees.
C. Carry out second and third tucks using the same technique as the first and with the strands in the same order (ie red, yellow, green).

C

D

E

D. Carry out three more tucks, always using the same technique but thinning the strands progressively by halving the number of yarns before each tuck; in this way, the splice will assume the characteristic tapered 'rat-tail' shape.

E. Completed eye splice. The ends of the strands have been removed with an electric cutter or with a soft iron knife heated over a flame.

109

A

B

Rope-to-wire splice

A. The first step consists in tapering the end of the wire that is to be inserted in the rope.
B. To do this, unlay the strands of wire one at a time, cutting each one off progressively further up the wire.
C. Having obtained an evenly tapered length, bind it tightly with adhesive tape and slip a metal fid onto the end as a temporary measure to facilitate insertion into the core of the rope.

C

D

D. Now prepare the rope. Tie a slipknot at a distance of three or four yards (3–4 m) from the end of the rope and uncover the core by pushing back the outer braid against the knot. Shorten the core by cutting off an 8–10 in (20–25 cm) length (do not forget this operation as otherwise the braid, when slid forward again, will not cover the finished splice). Insert the wire, capped by the fid, into the core to a distance of approximately 5 ft (1.5 m).

E   **F**

Rope-to-wire splice cont.

E. Push the fid out of the side of the core as shown in the photograph. Remove the fid and bind the core tightly around the wire rope, having first carefully smoothed out all creases and wrinkles.

F. Bind the core with tape at a distance of approximately 1 ft (30 cm) from its end and unravel the yarns. Group yarns into three equal bunches, taping the end of each bunch.

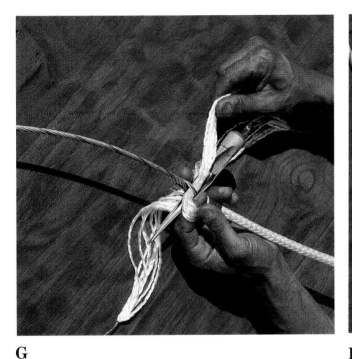

G

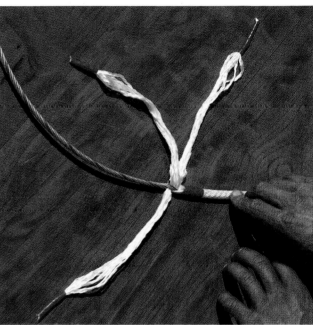

H

G. Insert the fid under two strands of wire, from right to left, and tuck the first bunch of fibres as shown in the photograph.
H. Tuck the other two bunches, progressing along the upper half of the wire and taking great care not to move the seventh strand, which is the core. As you have no doubt already realised, each bunch is wound repeatedly around the same pair of strands, enveloping them in a sheath of yarn.

Consequently, if the splice has been well executed, the wire will be covered completely and evenly by the yarns of the rope core.

I

L

Rope-to-wire splice cont.

I. Having completed the first three tucks, thin out each bunch by halving the number of yarns (to obtain a taper effect) and then carry out a further three tucks as described in H above.

L. This is how the completed core splice should look. Cut off loose ends with a knife (not with the electric cutter!) and pull the outer braid of the rope firmly down over the complete splice. The length of braid which extends beyond the existing splice must be unravelled into three bunches of yarns as in the case of the core.

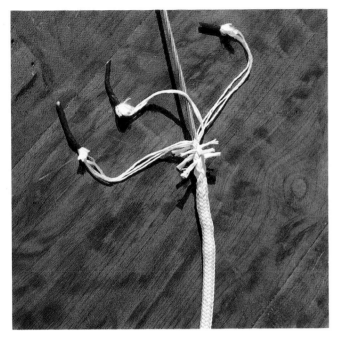

M

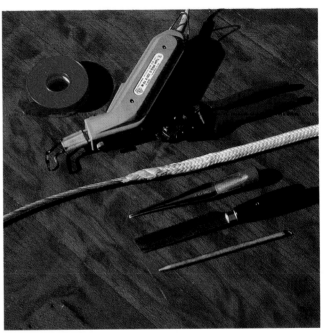

N

M. Splicing the braid onto the wire rope is done by the same technique as for the core, except that in this case the thinning of the three bunches is done progressively, starting from the fourth tuck and eliminating a few yarns at each stage so as to finish with three or four yarns in each bunch at the end of the final tuck.

N. Finish off the splice by removing all loose ends with the electric cutter, smear the completed splice with a little wax and rub vigorously between the palms of your hands to make the splice more compact.

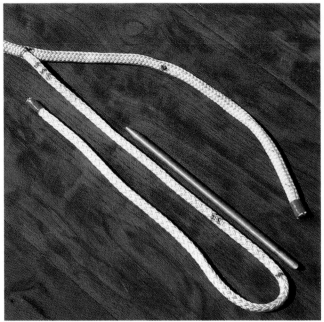

A

B

Splices: eye splice in plaited double-braid rope

A. Tie a slipknot at a distance of approximately 5 ft (1.5 m) from end of rope. Measure the length of a needle from end of the rope and mark this point with a large dot. Bend back the rope and form the desired size of eye with one end of the eye coinciding with the dot. Mark the other end of the eye on the opposite section of rope with an X.

B. Spread the yarns of the outer braid well apart at X and, with the help of a pusher, pull out the length of core from X to the end of the rope. Make a first reference mark (1) on the core at the point where it comes out at X. Continue to pull out the core at X until you have extracted a second length equal to the short section of a fid (the distance from rear end of fid to the two notches on the side of the light-alloy casing); make a second reference mark (2) on the core at the point

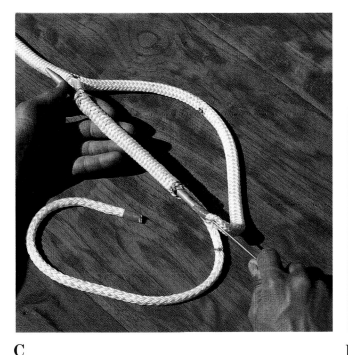

C

D

where it emerges at X. Continue to pull out the core at X until you have extracted a third length equal to the length of a fid; make a third reference mark (3) on the core at the point where it emerges at X.

C. Cut the end of the outer braid at an angle so that it will fit into the rear end of fid. Insert the fid into the core at reference mark (2) and, with the help of a pusher, push it along so that it drags in the outer braid; when the fid point has reached reference mark (3), push the point of the fid out of the core. (If the eye is to be looped around a snap shackle, ring, etc, slip this onto the outer braid before carrying out the operation described in this paragraph.)

D. Continue to push the fid so that, before it emerges completely from the core at reference mark (3), it has dragged the outer braid to the point where the dot on the braid is level with reference mark (2) on the core. The end of the outer braid protruding from the core at reference mark (3) is then tapered (by progressive thinning) in order to facilitate the next operation.

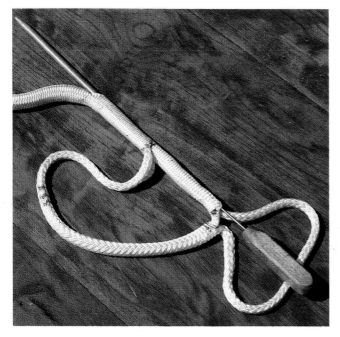

E

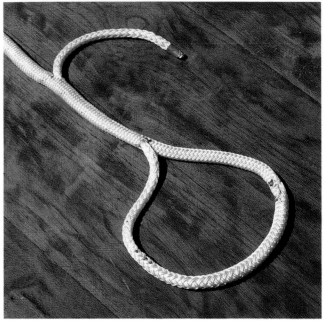

F

Splices: eye splice in plaited double-braid rope cont.

E. The tapered end of the outer braid is tucked into the core as shown in the photograph. The loose end of the core must now be re-inserted into the outer braid. This is done with the help of a fid inserted into the braid at the dot and then pushed back (with a pusher) towards the X. The fid must emerge from the outer braid at a distance beyond the X equal to a short fid section (see photograph D).

F. This is how the eye looks upon completion of step E. The crossover point where the two braids are interlaced (reference mark 2) is visible on the right-hand side of the photograph. In order for the next operation to proceed smoothly and without any problems, I would advise you to stitch the two braids together with waxed yarn, using a sailmaker's needle, from reference mark 2 to 3, and then back again to 2. In this way, the core and the outer braid inside it will form into one compact mass.

G

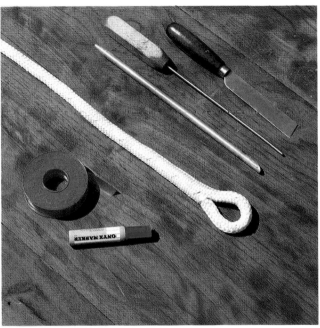

H

G. It is now necessary to 'milk' the outer braid, starting from the slipknot (which can be looped over a convenient projection) and progressing towards the X. Under the pressure of your fingers, the outer braid will edge downwards and the core retract into the braid, progressively narrowing the eye. The 'milking' must be continued until the crossover point (reference mark 2) has reached the X and disappeared into the outer braid. This is perhaps the most delicate stage of the entire splicing operation.

H. This is how the completed eye splice should look. There is one final operation, however, to be carried out: the loose end of the core protruding from the rope has to be unravelled and tapered (by progressive thinning) and the strands tucked back into the outer braid.

119

A

B

Splices: joining two ropes of different diameters

A. Make a slipknot about 6 ft (2 m) from the end of the larger rope and extract a good length of rope core. Wind tape firmly round the core at a distance of approximately 10–12 in (25–30 cm) from the end and cut off surplus length.

B. Sew the end of the shortened core to the end of the smaller rope (as shown in photograph), using waxed yarn and a sailmaker's needle.

C

D

C. Slide the outer braid of the larger rope down to the join and beyond it for a distance of 10–12 in (25–30 cm) (corresponding to the length of core cut off at step A). Taper the loose end of the braid (by progressively thinning out the yarns) and tape end tightly. Using a sailmaker's needle and waxed yarn, sew the splice from one end to the other (in both directions) with the type of stitch shown in the photograph. This will make the splice more compact.

D. Finish off the job by serving the splice tightly with waxed yarn.

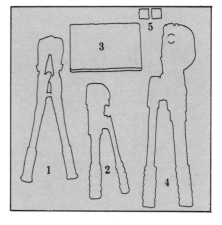

TOOLS FOR SPLICING WIRE ROPE

Legend:

1. Nicopress swaging calipers for ferrule sizes up to 5.5 mm. **2.** Norseman portable hydraulic wire-cutters which can cut through wire up to 20 mm in diameter. **3.** Kit of assorted ferrules. **4.** Norseman portable hydraulic press for ferrule sizes up to 12 mm, used with interchangeable dies, one pair for each size. **5.** Pair of interchangeable dies for Norseman portable hydraulic press.

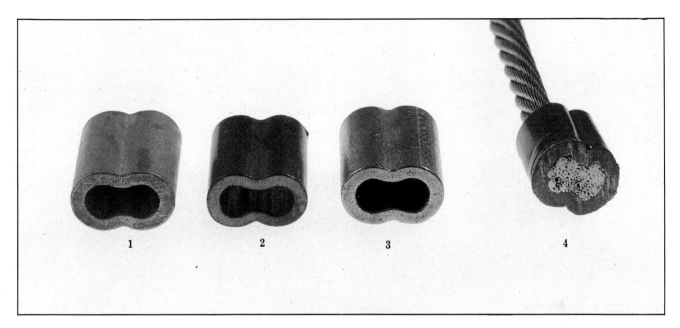

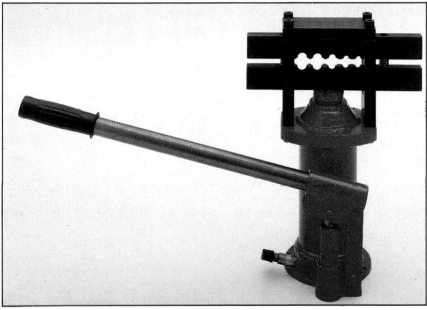

Above: Nicopress ferrules. *1*. Cadmium-plated copper ferrule. *2*. Copper ferrule. *3*. Nickel-plated copper ferrule. *4*. Cross-sectional view of pressed sleeve, showing even distribution of the wires over the cross-section.

Left: Douglas Marine hydraulic press for wire splicing. The special alloy-steel multiple die can press any size of ferrule in the 2–6 mm range with only a few strokes of the handle.

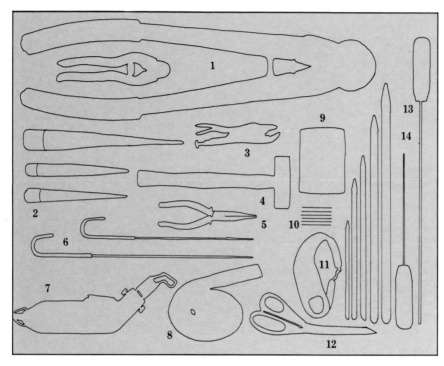

1. The large model cuts flexible steel wire up to 16 mm in diameter; the small model cuts flexible steel wire ropes up to 7 mm in diameter. 2. Types and sizes vary depending on the job. The two upper spikes are used for splicing laid three-strand ropes; the remaining spike has a flat tip and is particularly well suited for wire-to-rope splices. 3. This is the smallest size and is extremely useful for many types of work; the larger size should also be kept on board. 4. A mallet, which can be of wood, leather or even synthetic, is essential for all work involving wire or rope. 5. Check that the pliers have a wide enough gap. 6. These tools are used on double-braid ropes. 7. The best model on the market is the one shown in the illustration; made by Engel in Germany, it is very rugged and has interchangeable blades. 8. Choose a type of tape that is soft and has a uniform weave. 9/10/11/12. See page 22 (items 7, 5, 4, 1). 13/14. These long needles, also called fids, can be made of alloy or plastic; the size of the fid corresponds to the diameter of the rope on which it is to be used. The pushers, as the name indicates, are for pushing in the fids.

THE TOOLS OF
CHAPTER 5

Legend:

1. Felco wire-cutters. 2. Fids. 3. Adjustable grips. 4. Mallet. 5. Needle-nose pliers.
6. Special needles for splicing double-braid.
7. Portable electric rope cutter.
8. Tubular webbing. 9. Waxed twine.
10. Sailmaker's needles. 11. Sailmaker's palm. 12. Sailmaker's scissors.
13/14. Special tools for splicing plaited double-braid rope.

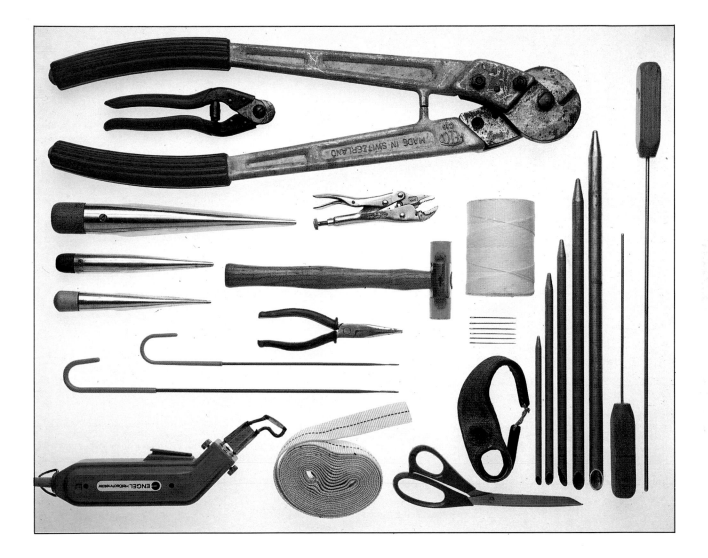

6. SAFETY ON BOARD

Safety measures are only too often neglected on pleasure craft; the subject is brought up periodically whenever some news item alarms public opinion, but the average yachtsman soon forgets all about it and does little or nothing to improve safety on board his boat.

At sea, safety is basically a question of mental attitude: it should be a constant subconscious concern of any sailor from the moment he sets foot on board, not just something to be remembered when a dangerous situation arises.

The best safety measure is prevention: don't wait until you run into trouble, but rather try to figure out beforehand what should be done in specific situations. Never postpone taking preventive measures; the sea is always unpredictable and ruthless and you can be sure that any mistake or negligence will cost you dear.

Let us take a look at some essential aids which help to ensure safety at sea.

LIFELINES

The role of lifelines is somewhat similar to that of the ropes enclosing a boxing ring; consequently, they need to be tough, resilient and capable of preventing you falling overboard should you lose your balance. Strong and sufficiently high lifelines are by themselves a big step forward in ensuring your safety on deck. Check the sturdiness of stanchions and wires and, if you have children on board, fix small-mesh netting to the lifelines all around the boat (see also Chapter 1).

Jack stays are an effective complement to lifelines; consisting of two (minimum diameter 6 mm) wires stretched along the deck, one

on each side, they enable the crew to go from one end of the boat to the other without unhitching their safety harnesses. It is important that jack stays should be installed in such a way that they will not interfere with or hamper work on deck; in addition, they should run

Below: jack stays should be rigged slightly above deck level to facilitate hitching-on the safety harness and should be sufficiently taut to prevent loss of balance when they are inadvertently trodden on. *left*: 3 ft (90 cm) high pulpit and triple lifelines; an extremely important safety feature.

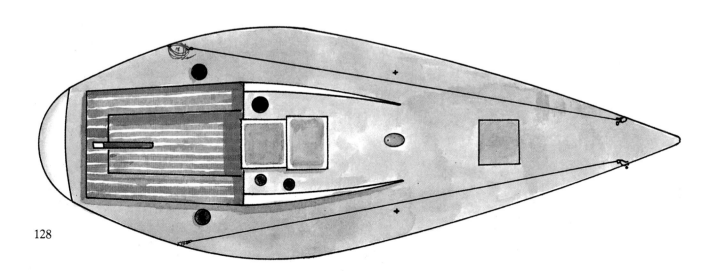

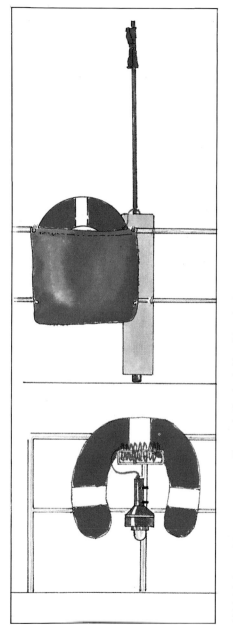

far enough aft so that it is possible to hitch onto them before leaving the cockpit and also permit reaching the bows without any need to detach oneself.

LIFEBUOYS AND FLOATING LIGHTS

There should be at least two lifebuoys of the horseshoe type on board, each capable of supporting the weight of a full-grown man and marked clearly with the name of the boat. Lifebuoys should be fitted with floating lights and should be stowed in such a way that they can be thrown overboard immediately in case of emergency. Check that the line joining the floating light to the lifebuoys is properly coiled and cannot get tangled as you are throwing it into the sea.

Stow all lifebuoys below deck during the winter months and re-

Two different arrangements for stowing lifebuoys. *Above*: the lifebuoy is placed in a canvas bag and tied to the dan buoy; the latter is housed in a piece of grey PVC pipe (of the type commonly used in the building trade) lashed to the pushpit. *Below*: the lifebuoy rests in a holder attached to the pushpit and is tied to the floating light with floating line.

move the batteries from the floating lights; incidentally, as an added precaution, replace batteries with new ones at least once a year.

A useful lifebuoy accessory is a dan buoy which is connected to the lifebelt by a 15–20 ft (5–6 m) long floating rope.

RADAR REFLECTOR

Although radar reflectors are generally considered indispensable only in the case of single-handed sailing, they are in fact also extremely useful for ordinary cruising. If you do not want to use the paint mentioned in Chapter 1, you can use the standard alloy reflector; but remember that this must be installed externally in an unobstructed position.

The normal location for the reflector is suspended from the crosstrees, but in that position it often interferes with the running rigging and can also cause damage to the sails. An alternative solution is to install it at the masthead, but in this case care must be taken to choose a model which is sufficiently compact not to obstruct any other masthead equipment.

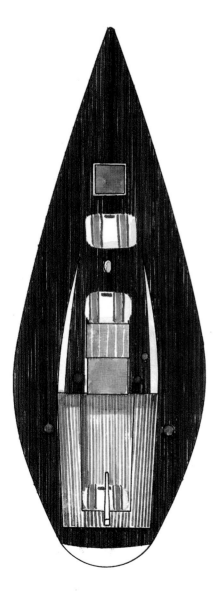

INFLATABLE LIFERAFT

Time after time, in visiting other boats, I have noticed that the rip cord of the inflatable liferaft is not secured externally in any way but, on the contrary, is neatly coiled and stowed away in its compartment. Make quite sure, therefore, that the rip cord of your raft is attached by a strop to some solid piece of deck equipment; failing this, or if the raft is stowed in a locker (where it must be easily accessible), fix a strong eye to the deck alongside the locker or wherever the raft is lashed down.

Inflatable liferafts must be inspected and overhauled periodically, according to the manufacturer's instructions and only by competent, authorised firms that specialise in this type of work.

A final warning: make quite sure, before leaving your boat, that you have got a knife for cutting the rip cord. And remember, too, that even if damaged your boat may still be the safest place; so think twice before leaving it!

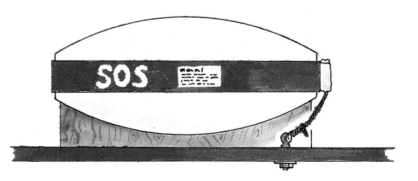

Above: the figure shows the rip cord of a life raft tied to a nearby eye bolt (more reliable than a normal eye plate). *Left*: three possible locations for stowing the inflatable liferaft on deck. Selection of the most appropriate solution depends on the deck layout of the boat, the number of crew and the best weight distribution.

COMPANIONWAY

During a storm or in a very rough sea, you must be able to close off the companionway so as to prevent water flooding the interior of the boat. Wash boards should be of solid construction to withstand the weight of water slamming against them and should be stowed within easy reach. In addition, it is essential for the sliding hatch cover to be fitted with some kind of latch so that it cannot be opened accidentally by waves sweeping the deck.

CHAIN LOCKER

Since the forepeak is often used as a chain locker, its hatch cover must be fitted with a strong reliable latch so that it cannot be opened by a heavy sea taken on board, with consequent dangerous escape of anchor and/or chain onto the deck. In rough weather, and especially when sailing close-hauled in a heavy sea, it is advisable to remove the anchor from the bows and stow it in a locker, or even below deck, since if by any chance it breaks loose it becomes a lethal weapon and can even stave in the bows of the boat.

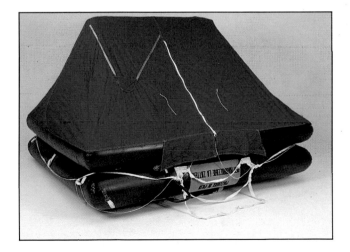

Above: EPIRB, a small portable emergency radio transmitter which acts as a beacon, giving the position of a craft in distress in the open sea. Pocket-sized and reasonably priced, it has a fairly long range and is an invaluable asset for anyone who sails far from land.
Right: inflatable liferaft with protective canopy. The type illustrated cannot be steered, but other types are currently being tried out which can be steered and offer the undoubted advantage of so-called 'dynamic survival'.

SAFETY HARNESSES

The models and makes of yacht safety harness on the market are legion, but very few of them are really effective. A good harness must be easy to put on, simple in design and structurally very strong. Remember that it often has to be donned over oilskins so the size should be big enough to accommodate this somewhat bulky equipment.

Two items of the harness must always be checked with particular care: the hook and the line. Do not trust nylon lines which are too springy and often have suspect splices; choose instead tough polyester rope or even a strap, as long as it has good stout seams. The hook must be of AISI 316 stainless steel, with a breaking load of at least 2,600 lb (1,200 kg). Remember that the hook must be attached only to a firmly anchored deck fitting and never, for example, to a stanchion or lifeline.

In bad weather, the helmsman is the first who must don a harness and hitch himself on, since with both hands on the wheel you cannot have 'one hand for the boat and one for yourself'.

Life jackets, too, should be loose-fitting and easy to don; they should be stowed in easily accessible lockers so that they can be put on rapidly in an emergency.

Yachtsmen who sail during the winter months or in cold waters should consider the advantages of having on board a number of survival suits; these one-piece neoprene suits are practically watertight and enable a person to survive in extremely cold and even ice-bound waters. The cost of these suits is still rather high, but is fully justified by their remarkable effectiveness which has saved a great many lives in recent years.

The survival suit, unfortunately still rather highly priced, can be put on in a few seconds over oilskins, is watertight, buoyant and in no way hampers movement around the deck.

7. MAKING READY FOR AN OCEAN CROSSING

Is there anyone who has not dreamed at some time of cutting loose and heading off on a long sea voyage? Generations of seafarers have been lured by the fascination of the unknown to respond to the irresistible call of the ocean – and to remain forever under the spell of its mysterious magic.

Crossing an ocean today has lost much of its allure, partly because hundreds of boats sail across the Atlantic every year; but nevertheless it still remains a challenge, and an exacting one which should never be undertaken lightly or with insufficient preparation.

If you are one of those who have decided to transform dream into reality, here is some advice on how to set about it.

IS YOUR BOAT UP TO IT?

Some years ago, at Puerto Rico in the Canary Islands, I ran across a most unusual type of craft that was being made ready to cross the Atlantic to the Antilles: this was an amphibious Volkswagen Beetle specially modified for the purpose. The driver (one could hardly call him a helmsman) was fully confident that his 'vessel' was perfectly capable of making the voyage. My own boat left shortly afterwards and I never managed to find out what happened to this eccentric character and his strange craft.

Obviously this was a special case (and as such not to be imitated!). As far as the suitability of your own boat is concerned, the criteria for making a critical judgement must be based above all on the route you plan to take, and on the wind and wave conditions you will probably meet along your chosen course. Collect as much information as you can, with the help of books, charts, sailing directions and other publications available at specialist bookshops. For example, it is true that crossing to the Caribbean in the trade wind belt is comparatively easy (for one thing,

one is on a run the whole way); but it is equally true that the return journey will be hard going, sailing most of the time close-hauled into a head sea which, at times, becomes quite rough. Keep in mind that during ocean passages both hull and rigging are inevitably subjected to severe stressing; you may quite well find yourself compelled to sail close-hauled for an entire week, always on the same tack, with a 25–30 knot apparent wind and a heavy swell. Under these conditions, the hull, the sails and all the rigging have to withstand prolonged, intense and continuous stresses and must therefore possess qualities of maximum toughness and resilience.

MAST AND STANDING RIGGING

Particular care must be taken in fitting out and checking this vital equipment. Check the whole mast thoroughly, above all the welds and stay anchorages, for signs of wear or fatigue. Bolts, nuts and split pins must be in perfect condition and protected with silicone; masthead sheaves must revolve smoothly and be well lubricated; instruments and other gear mounted at the masthead must be

fastened firmly in place and be fully operational, since carrying out repairs under way is a long and difficult operation. If you have any spare sheaves at the masthead, reeve them with strong messengers as they will prove extremely useful if and when you have to replace a halyard. It is also a good idea to take a spare halyard with you, of a type that can be adapted to serve either the mainsail or the genoa.

If only a basic bosun's chair is normally kept on board, add one of the more elaborate types that are suitable for use at sea.

The best standing rigging for long-range cruising is 1 × 19 wire; not only does this type of rigging possess adequate flexibility, but it also gives early warning of fatigue (generally by an untwisting of the strands). Make sure that you have a few easily fitted terminals of the right diameter to fit your wire so that you can deal rapidly with any problems in this department.

If your mast has double spreaders but is not fitted with babystay and runners, it might be advisable to modify the rig to include these features; they really contribute substantially to steadying the middle section of the mast against the vibrations set up by the hull slam-

ming into the waves when sailing close-hauled in a heavy sea, especially under shortened sail. If necessary, ask the advice of an experienced friend. For the runners, it is essential to fit a system that prevents the lee runner from swinging about when not in use (see Chapter 3).

The tips of the spreaders must be adequately protected and it is advisable also to pad the aft lower shrouds to prevent them from wearing out the mainsail when the boat is on a dead run with the boom squared off and the mainsail pressing against the shrouds.

Boom hardware and reefing gear must be made as efficient as possible. During a long cruise you will be compelled to take in and shake out reefs over and over again, and it is important that one person should be able to do this on his own without undue strain and without leaving the cockpit (see Chapter 4). If your mainsail has

Mast and rigging should be inspected at regular intervals during long cruises. In the photograph, a crew member has been hauled aloft to check the spreaders. Other critical items which should be checked regularly are the connections of rigging to the mast.

Sail repair kit

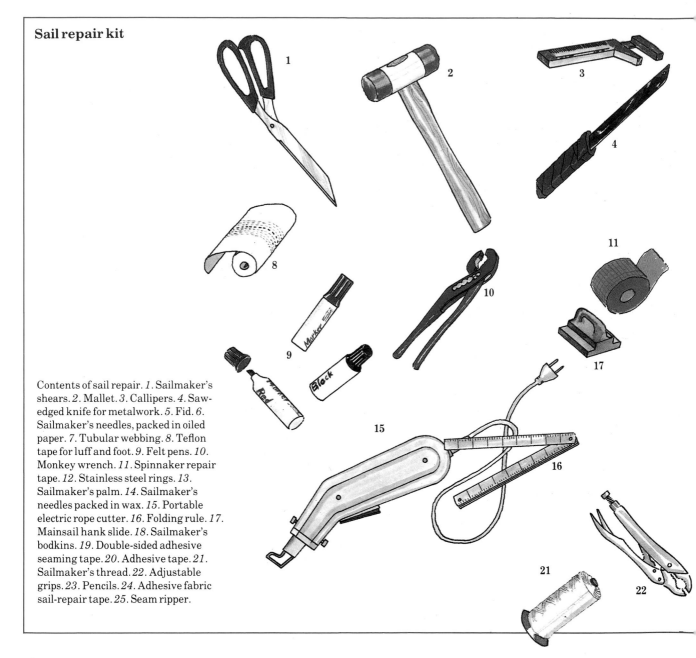

Contents of sail repair. *1*. Sailmaker's shears. *2*. Mallet. *3*. Callipers. *4*. Saw-edged knife for metalwork. *5*. Fid. *6*. Sailmaker's needles, packed in oiled paper. *7*. Tubular webbing. *8*. Teflon tape for luff and foot. *9*. Felt pens. *10*. Monkey wrench. *11*. Spinnaker repair tape. *12*. Stainless steel rings. *13*. Sailmaker's palm. *14*. Sailmaker's needles packed in wax. *15*. Portable electric rope cutter. *16*. Folding rule. *17*. Mainsail hank slide. *18*. Sailmaker's bodkins. *19*. Double-sided adhesive seaming tape. *20*. Adhesive tape. *21*. Sailmaker's thread. *22*. Adjustable grips. *23*. Pencils. *24*. Adhesive fabric sail-repair tape. *25*. Seam ripper.

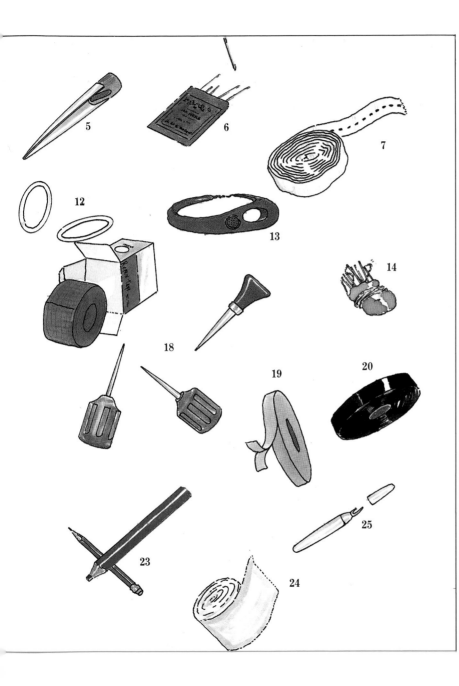

5
6
7
12
13
14
18
19
20
23
24
25

Above: needles, thread, a sailmaker's palm and a bit of patience are all that is required for minor repairs to a sail. For long-range cruising, however, it is preferable to have a sewing machine on board which gives better results in considerably less time.

Bosun's chair permits freedom of movement in complete safety; it is however rather uncomfortable and not very suitable for long stays aloft.

only two sets of reef cringles, put in a third and pass a messenger through the two upper cringles to facilitate reeving the upper reef pennant when it is needed (see Chapter 5). All shackle pins should be secured with steel wire and the pin ends protected with adhesive tape.

Finally, always keep a few extra blocks and snatch-blocks on board, as well as a range of spare shackles.

SAILS

Your sails are bound to be driven hard during a long sea crossing so, before leaving port, every precaution should be taken to limit as far as possible the inevitable wear.

Areas where the sail is apt to chafe against the rigging must be reinforced by sewing on extra thicknesses of sail cloth. Two common places for sail wear are the genoa foot, which rubs against the pulpit in a following wind, and the parts of the leech that are level with the spreaders and chafe against them during hoisting and tacking.

Mainsail seams should be covered on both sides with adhesive sail-repair tape to protect them against salt spray and ultra-violet rays as well as wear resulting from continual chafing against rigging and spreaders. The reef cringles also deserve close attention, since they are continually put under high stress; they can be made more secure by lashing with tubular webbing. A wise precaution is to put a couple of strong stitches into the batten pockets so that the battens cannot fall out accidentally; it is also advisable to take a few spare battens with you.

Long-range cruising should never be attempted without having on board a complete kit for repairing sails (see illustration), together with an adequate stock of spare pieces of sailcloth in the same weights as your sails.

Other essential items include a set of cringles for the mainsail, a set of hanks for the foresails, at least 20 yards (20 m) of tubular tape and a few strong steel rings.

Sail protection

A foresail with reinforcing pieces of adhesive sailcloth at the points of major wear (ie where the sail frets against spreader tips, pulpit, stanchions). The mainsail is protected by covering the seams with adhesive fabric tape.

RUNNING RIGGING

Inspect halyards, sheets and any other rope used for working the sails and replace any worn or doubtful cordage; lay in a sufficient supply of the harder-worked types and sizes of rope and make a thorough inspection of the deck to determine at which points the ropes are more likely to suffer wear. Remember that, once out at sea, you may have to keep the same sail trim for days on end and that even the slightest fretting of a sheet against some object on deck can cause premature failure of the rope.

Remedial action consists in careful alignment of all deck fittings for the running rigging and in protecting, with duct tape or leather strips, the points of potential contact. During ocean crossings, a tour of inspection of the deck is usually made at least once every 24 hours; by observing this wise practice you will find that you save yourself a lot of bother.

If you have a second spinnaker pole, take it with you, well lashed down on deck, as it could prove useful if you run into trouble: for instance, breakage of spinnaker pole or main boom, dismasting, etc.

RIGGING

This seems a good moment to advise against the practice (so dear, to judge by their writings, to many lone or nearly-lone yachtsmen) of setting twin staysails on spinnaker poles. In my opinion, this rig is the most inconvenient and clumsy imaginable; it involves lowering the mainsail and running straight before the wind, with very uncomfortable results as the boat frequently wallows violently and loses a lot of speed. In addition, setting the sails is a complicated business and, if the wind freshens or there is a sudden squall, lowering them rapidly is equally, if not more difficult.

If you do not want to use the spinnaker, the ideal rig consists of mainsail plus a medium jib, bent to the forestay and boomed out with

By using a spinnaker sock, developed by single-handed sailors, even a skeleton crew can handle this sail. There are two main types of sock: the one consisting in a series of rings (shown in the photograph) and the other, more practical, shaped like a sleeve. The second type must have rather a wide, stiff mouth and be made of light but strong fabric; the sock downhaul must be a strong, small-diameter rope which does not kink easily; in fact, under certain wind conditions, it may be necessary to lead it to a winch for hauling down the sock.

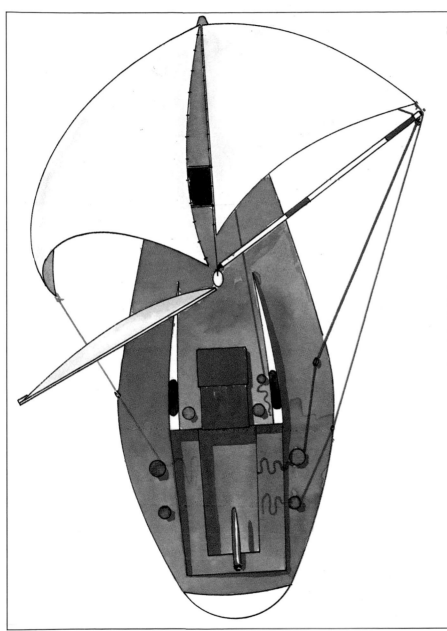

Sail plan for following winds

A valid alternative to the traditional twin staysail rig. A medium-size genoa is set on the weather side, bent to the forestay and boomed out with the spinnaker pole; a large flying genoa, with tack made fast to the bows, is then hoisted to leeward using the spinnaker halyard. The system for trimming the spinnaker boom consists of topping lift, downhaul and guy, the last two made fast together to the lower ring on the pole end. The genoa sheet is reeved through the jaws of the end fitting. With this system the boomed-out genoa can be gybed with the spinnaker pole still in position. To change tack, work the sails as follows:

(i) lower flying genoa to leeward; (ii) move boomed-out genoa over to the lee side and lower spinnaker pole on deck; (iii) trim both genoa and mainsail on new tack; (iv) hoist spinnaker pole into position on new tack; (v) set flying genoa to windward.

the spinnaker pole, and a flying genoa sheeted to leeward with the tack made fast at the bows. Should the wind freshen suddenly, all you have to do is to let go the genoa sheet, drop the genoa at the bows (in the same way as a blooper) and reef the mainsail; in a few minutes the boat is ready to weather even a moderate gale. In addition, with this rig you will be compelled to sail with the wind on the quarter between 120 and 150 degrees off the wind (ie on the fastest point of sailing), wearing to change tack at regular intervals. Apart from the advantage of periodically relieving the strain on the rigging on each side, more stability is obtained as a result of the increase in speed and the more equal fore-and-aft distribution of the sail area.

STEERING SYSTEM

A general inspection of the steering system is essential if you want to avoid unpleasant surprises during your voyage. Check that the free play of the rudder is not excessive and that the quadrant is firmly seated and fastened in place. Make sure that the sheaves revolve freely and are lubricated and that there is a pair of spare steering cables on board, ready for instant use in case of failure. Check that you have an emergen-

cy tiller which can be fitted onto or into the rudder-stock if the wheel steering system fails. If your boat is fitted with a tiller instead of a wheel, it is sufficient to check the amount of play of the rudder and the connection of the tiller to the rudderstock; in this case, too, it is advisable to carry a spare tiller on board.

Wind-vane self-steering gear is of great help in the open sea and, although rather expensive, deserves serious consideration for long-range cruising. From the

With the wind on the quarter, the course is maintained by the self-steering gear (the wind vane is visible at the centre of the photograph).

many models available on the market, choose the one which is most suitable for your boat in terms of size, ruggedness and method of installation to the hull. Distrust excessively complicated models as they are almost always a source of trouble. Make a careful study of the route of the control lines to the wheel or tiller, and incorporate a system for quick release.

If your boat has a means of generating electricity, you can go one better and install an automatic pilot. The only drawback with this type of device is that, if it gets damaged, repairs are often difficult. For that reason, make quite sure that the control unit is well protected from salt spray and that it is correctly set to operate in prevailing wind and wave conditions.

If you cannot afford an automatic steering system, you can always fall back on the old-fashioned but well-tested shock cord method. Keep a few lengths of different-diameter shock cord on board and resign yourself to be patient, since this method requires precise trimming of the sails, repeated experiment and a definite 'feel' for the behaviour of your boat.

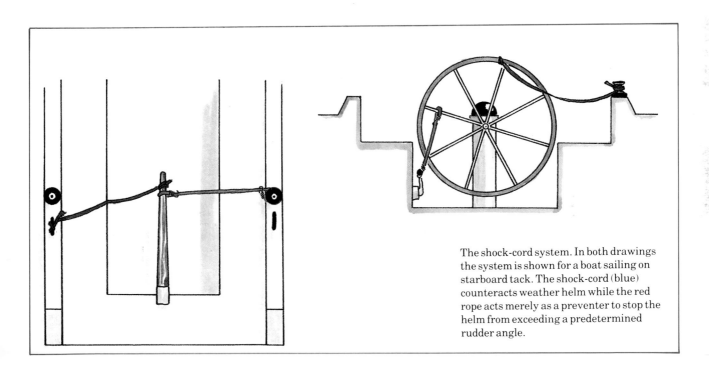

The shock-cord system. In both drawings the system is shown for a boat sailing on starboard tack. The shock-cord (blue) counteracts weather helm while the red rope acts merely as a preventer to stop the helm from exceeding a predetermined rudder angle.

RIGGING

SAFETY

Maximum attention must be given to all aspects of safety, since you will often find yourself up against unexpected situations – or at any rate ones that are new to you. Above all, remember that the safety of your boat and of its crew depends solely on you, on your awareness of your own limitations and capabilities.

If you are contemplating an ocean crossing, all the provisions discussed in Chapter 6 are to be considered mandatory, with the following additions.

Inflatable liferaft

At the time of its service, the raft should be equipped with a supply of drinking water, emergency food rations and essential survival gear (clasp knife, lanyard, signalling mirror, paddle, radar reflector, fishing line and hooks, etc). Most firms specialising in the overhaul of life rafts offer this service, as well as a list of optional items which can be included in the raft depending on the requirements of the client.

Survival kit

Prepare a number of watertight plastic containers for ship's papers and other documents, for valuables, for drinking water and emergency food rations, for fishing tackle, Very lights and any other item which you think might be useful for survival on an inflatable raft. Tie the containers to each other with a lanyard and stow them where they can be easily reached in the case of an emergency. Radio transmitters which send SOS signals at regular intervals on predetermined frequencies are highly recommended; rugged, watertight and buoyant, they reduce to a minimum the risk of drifting undetected for weeks on end. Another very useful accessory in this respect is the portable VHF set, which enables you to communicate with passing ships with infinitely more chance of success than the traditional flares. The figure shows a range of basic survival equipment, which can be supplemented according to individual preferences and requirements. *1.* Drinking water. *2.* Documents. *3.* Personal medicines. *4.* Metal foil. *5/6.* Ropes. *7.* Clasp-knife. *8.* Salt. *9.* Anti-sunburn cream. *10.* Sunglasses. *11.* Mirror. *12.* Anti-seasickness pills. *13.* Mug. *14.* Matches. *15.* Desalinator. *16.* Portable automatic radio transmitter. *17.* VHF set. *18.* Fishing tackle. *19.* Tinned food.

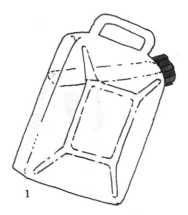

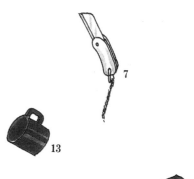

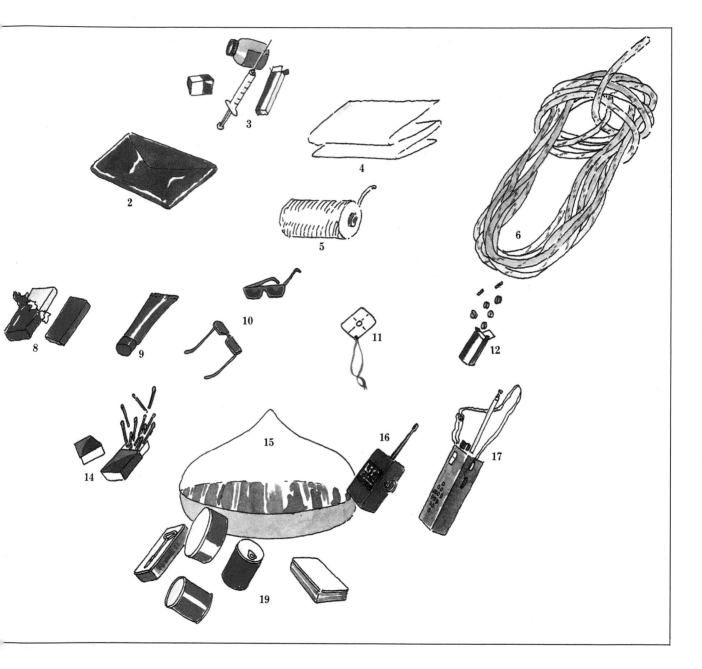

Chain locker

Empty the locker completely and stow anchor and chain in the bilges at the centre of the boat. In this way the bows will be lightened considerably and the boat's trim and performance will benefit. The resulting empty space can be used for storing fenders or anything light which does not mind being damp.

If there is no watertight bulwark between locker and accommodation, make sure that the hawse pipe can be plugged (as shown in figure) to prevent the ingress of water.

Safety harnesses

There must be one harness for each crew member. The helmsman must always be the first to put on a harness as he has both hands occupied and is therefore more liable to be swept overboard.

CONCLUSION

Preparing for ocean voyage requires above all a certain talent for organisation and puts to the test one of the principal characteristics of the blue-water sailor: the capacity to foresee what could happen in the immediate future and to ready both himself and his boat in time to meet any eventuality. Acquire all the information you can, consulting books and other publications and talking to anyone who has already personally undergone a similar experience.

A word about choosing your crew. It is useless to own the perfect boat if you are unable to enjoy her owing to an unhappy atmosphere on board. Sailing literature is full of disastrous examples of cruises which have come to a premature end owing to violent quarrels and clashes of personality – and on an ocean voyage there is the added difficulty that ports for disembarkation are usually few and far between.

Finally, remember that once you have weighed anchor you have only yourself and your own resources to rely on and that nearly all the classic landfalls of long cruises are idyllic places with azure seas and white beaches, where sailmakers, yacht chandlers and shops selling nautical equipment have still to be invented. So provide yourself with sunglasses and sun creams, and may you have a fair wind.

Hawse pipe plug. An essential item for long range cruising, the plug can be made of hard rubber or of wood. A wooden plug gives a better seal, since it swells when wet. The end of the chain should be tied to the plug, as shown in the figure; in this way, the chain can be hauled back on deck when the plug is removed and in addition the weight of the chain will hold the plug firmly in position when inserted.
On opposite page: Marigot Bay in St Lucia in the Caribbean. White beaches, blue sea, luxuriant vegetation, the perfect ending for a long ocean crossing.

Legend

1. Baby stay. **2.** Halyard exit. **3.** Organizer. **4.** Fairlead blocks. **5.** Stanchion. **6.** Genoa car. **7.** Pad eye. **8.** Swivel lead block. **9.** Genoa track. **10.** Turning block. **11.** Cleat. **12.** Snatch block. **13.** Back stay adjuster. **14.** Back stay. **15.** Traveller main sheet. **16.** Sheet stopper. **17.** Mainsheet purchase. **18.** Kicker. **19.** Forestay. **20.** Runners.

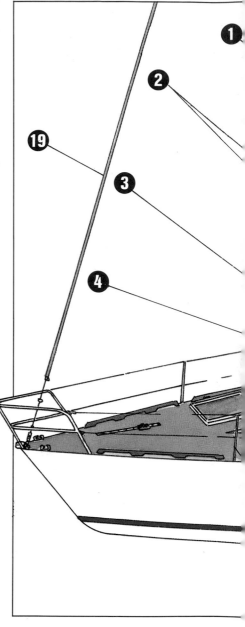

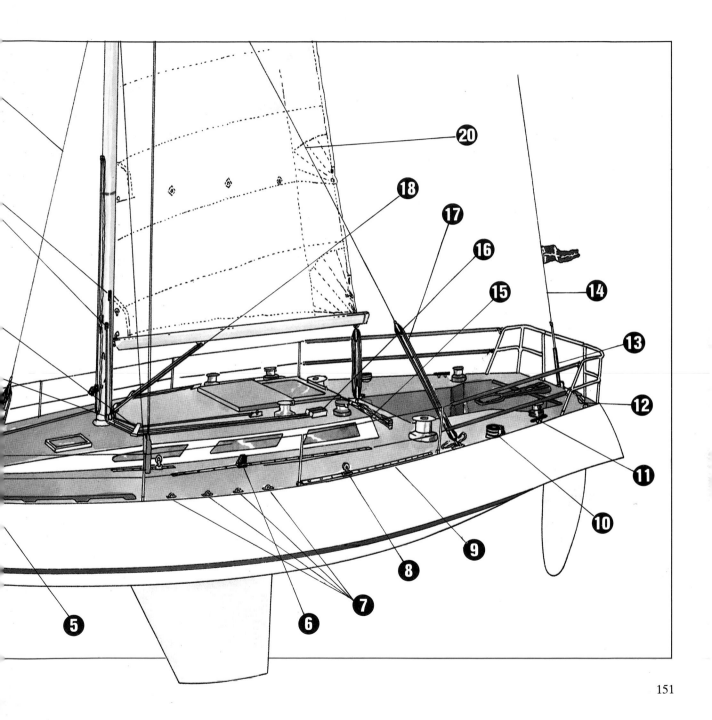